CERTIFICATION CIRCLE™

MOUS

Microsoft Outlook 2002

Marjorie Hunt

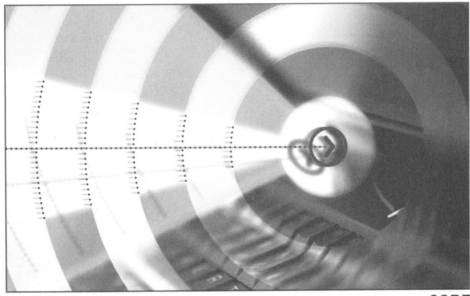

CORE

MICROSOFT OFFICE
USER SPECIALIST

Microsoft®
OFFICE

APPROVED COURSEWARE

THOMSON
━━★━━
COURSE TECHNOLOGY™

Australia • Canada • Mexico • Singapore • Spain • United Kingdom • United States

MOUS Microsoft Outlook 2002

CERTIFICATION CIRCLE™ *CORE*

Marjorie Hunt

Managing Editor:
Nicole Jones Pinard

Product Manager:
Julia Healy

Editorial Assistant:
Elizabeth Harris

Production Editor:
Debbie Masi

Contributing Author:
Carol Cram

Developmental Editors:
Jane Hosie-Bounar,
Kim Crowley

Composition House:
GEX Publishing Services

QA Manuscript Reviewers:
Nicole Ashton, Jeff Schwartz,
Alex White

Book Designers:
Joseph Lee, black fish design

Thank You, Advisory Board!

This book is a result of the hard work and dedication by authors, editors, and more than 30 instructors focused on Microsoft Office and MOUS certification. These instructors formed our Certification Circle Advisory Board. We looked to them to flesh out our original vision and turn it into a sound pedagogical method of instruction. In short, we asked them to partner with us to create *the* book for preparing for a MOUS Exam. And, now we wish to thank them for their contributions and expertise.

ADVISORY BOARD MEMBERS:

Linda Amergo	Old Westbury
Shellie Besharse	Mississippi County Community College
Margaret Britt	Copiah Lincoln Community College
Becky Burt	Copiah Lincoln Community College
Judy Cameron	Spokane Community College
Elizabeth T. De Arazoza	Miami-Dade Community College
Susan Dozier	Tidewater Community College
Dawna Dewire	Babson College
Pat Evans	J. Sargent Reynolds
Susan Fry	Boise State University
Joyce Gordon	Babson College
Steve Gordon	Babson College
Pat Harley	Howard Community College
Rosanna Hartley	Western Piedmont Community College
Eva Hefner	St. Petersburg Junior College
Becky Jones	Richland College
Mali Jones	Johnson and Wales University
Angie McCutcheon	Washington State Community College
Barbara Miller	Indiana University
Carol Milliken	Kellogg Community College
Maureen Paparella	Monmouth University
Mike Puopolo	Bunker Hill Community College
Kathy Proittei	Essex Community College
Pamela M. Randall	Unicity Network
Theresa Savarese	San Diego City College
Barbara Sherman	Buffalo State
Kathryn Surles	Salem Community College
Beth Thomas	Hagerstown Community College
Barbara Webber	Northern Essex Community College
Jean Welsh	Lansing Community College
Lynn Wermers	North Shore Community College
Sherry Young	Kingwood College

Preface

Welcome to the *CERTIFICATION CIRCLE SERIES*. Each book in this series is designed with one thing in mind: preparing you to pass a Microsoft Office User Specialist (MOUS) exam. This strict focus allows you to target the skills you need to be successful. You will not need to study anything extra—it's like getting a peek at the exam before you take it! Read on to learn more about how the book is organized and how you will get the most out of it.

Table of Contents

This book is organized around the MOUS exam objectives. Each Skill on the exam is taught on two facing pages with text on the left and figures on the right. This also makes for a terrific reference; if you want to brush up on a few skills, it's easy to find the ones you're looking for.

Getting Started Chapter

Each book begins with a Getting Started Chapter. This Chapter contains skills that are *not* covered on the exam but the authors felt were vital to understanding the software. The content in this chapter varies from application to application.

Skill Overview

Each skill starts with a paragraph explaining the concept and how you would use it. These are clearly written and concise.

Skill Steps

The Steps required to perform the skill appear on the left page with what you type in green text.

Tips

We provide tips specific to the skill or how the skill is tested on the exam.

Skill Set 2

Scheduling

Add Appointments, Meetings, and Events to the Calendar

Schedule Resources for Meetings

Sometimes a meeting requires special equipment, such as a flip chart, a projector, or a monitor. You can use Outlook to reserve this kind of item, called a **resource**, for a meeting. To do this, you invite the resource you need to the meeting, just as you would invite a person. However, this feature is not available to everyone using Outlook. In order to schedule resources for a meeting, you must have Outlook running on a Microsoft Exchange Server. In addition, each resource you want to invite must have its own e-mailbox on the server. If both these requirements are met, then you can schedule resources. To schedule a resource, you use the Plan a Meeting form to set a time for your meeting, and then use the Select Attendees and Resources dialog box to choose the resources you want. You then use the Meeting Request form to invite all the attendees and resources to the meeting.

Activity Steps

tip

Sometimes, certain resources are restricted so that only a select group of people have the right to use them. If you try to schedule a resource you do not have permission to use, the resource will automatically reject your meeting request.

1. Click the Calendar icon 📅 on the Outlook Bar, if necessary, click **Actions** on the menu bar, then click **Plan a Meeting**

2. Click **Add Others**, then click **Add from Address Book**
   See Figure 2-7. If your school or company is connected to a Global Address List, you will see a list of resources in the Name list.

3. Click **Bettijean Riley** in the Name list, then click **Required**

4. If you see a list of Resources in the Name list, click one of the **Resources in the list, then click Resources** (If you don't see a list of resources, click one of the names, then click **Resources**)
   The e-mail address of the person responsible for the resource you clicked appears in the Resources box.

5. Click **OK** (If a dialog box opens asking if you want to join the Microsoft Office Internet Free/Busy Service, click **Cancel**.)

6. Use the horizontal scroll bar so that 3:00 tomorrow appears on the time grid, click **3:00**, then click **Make Meeting** at the bottom of the Plan a Meeting form

7. Type **Brainstorming meeting** in the Subject box, type **Siberian Conference Room** in the Location box, then click **Send**
   The Meeting form closes. The Plan a Meeting form shows the day of your newly planned meeting with the 3:00 time slot shaded in blue. *See Figure 2-8.*

8. Click **Close**, click tomorrow's date on the Date Navigator to view the new meeting, then click the **Today button** on the toolbar

Additional Projects

For those who want more practice applying the skills they've learned, there is a project for each skill set located at the back of each book. The projects ask you to combine the skills you've learned to create a meaningful document – just what you do in real life.

Project for Skill Set 2
Scheduling

Meeting Schedules for Pacific Imports

Pacific Imports is a small retail outlet based in Seattle, Washington that sells craft products from various Pacific Rim nations such as Japan, Malaysia, Australia, Chile, and Mexico. Meetings are held frequently to discuss new products and to plan marketing strategies. In this project, you will use Outlook to add appointments to the Calendar, schedule meetings and resources, and manage meeting requests for two managers at Pacific Imports: Derek Thirlwell and Shaun Richter, and for Rie Nishimura, who is in charge of Resources.

Activity Steps

1. In the Calendar, enter the appointment **Planning Meeting** at **3:00 pm** for tomorrow; the meeting will last **2 hours** and take place in the **Coral Reef Conference Room**

2. Create a new category called **Planning**, add the Planning meeting to the Planning category, make the meeting one that recurs every month on the same day (e.g., the first Tuesday), save and close the meeting, then apply a conditional format to the Planning Meeting that makes it a **Business** meeting based on the condition that **planning** appears in the subject

3. Schedule an all-day event for next Wednesday called **Employee Appreciation Day** that will take place at **Mayfair Roller Rink**; remove the reminder, show the time as **Out of Office**, label the meeting as **Must Attend**, include the text shown in **Figure OP 2-1**, then save and close the event

4. Schedule a meeting from **10:00** to **12:00** in the **Pacific Oasis Conference Room** on another free day in your calendar that uses **Rei Nishimura** as the Resource and discusses **Taiwan Imports**, with **Derek Thirlwell** and **Shaun Richter** as required attendees

5. In your Inbox, open the **Product Launch Meeting** message, accept the meeting request, edit the response by adding the message as shown in **Figure OP 2-2**, send a copy of the message to **Derek Thirlwell** and a copy to yourself, then view the meeting date in the calendar

6. Open the **New Zealand Conference** message in your Inbox, decline the meeting request with the message **I'm sorry, Derek, I need to be in Taiwan that week.**, open the **Australia Manager Meeting** message, propose a new meeting time of **1:00 pm** to **2:30 pm**, then send a copy of the message to yourself

7. Print all the appointments in the **Daily Style** for April 3, 2003

120   Certification Circle

Skill 1
Add Appointments, Meetings, and Events to the Calendar

Figure 2-7: Select Attendees and Resources dialog box

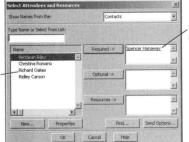

Your name should appear here

Any resources available to you will appear in this list

Figure 2-8: Plan a Meeting form with new meeting

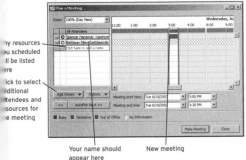

Any resources you scheduled will be listed here

Click to select additional attendees and resources for the meeting

Your name should appear here

New meeting

Figures
There are at least two figures per skill which serve as a reference as you are working through the steps. Callouts focus your attention to what's important.

Extra Boxes
This will *not* be on the exam–it's extra–hence the name. But, there are some very cool things you can do with Office xp so we had to put this stuff somewhere!

Target Your Skills
At the end of each unit, there are two Target Your Skills exercises. These require you to create a document from scratch, based on the figure, using the skills you've learned in the chapter. And, the solution is provided– there's no wasted time trying to figure out if you've done it right.

extra!

Using the Microsoft Office Free/Busy Service
If you have Internet access and would like to let others know when you have free blocks of time, you can publish your available and busy times to the Microsoft Office Internet Free/Busy Service, a Web-based service offered through Microsoft. Doing this lets other users of the service plan meetings and schedule a time that works for you. For more Information, visit http://freebusy. office.microsoft.com/ freebusy/freebusy.dll on the Web.

Microsoft Outlook 2002   **33**

Additional Resources

There are many resources available with this book—both free and for a nominal fee. Please see your sales representative for more information. The resources available with this book are:

INSTRUCTOR'S MANUAL

Available as an electronic file, the Instructor's Manual is quality-assurance tested and includes unit overviews, lecture topics, solutions to all lessons and projects, and extra Target Your Skills. The Instructor's Manual is available on the Instructor's Resource Kit CD-ROM, or you can download if from www.course.com.

FACULTY ONLINE COMPANION

You can browse this textbook's password protected site to obtain the Instructor's Manual, Solution Files, Project Files, and any updates to the text. Contact your Customer Service Representative for the site address and password.

PROJECT FILES

Project Files contain all of the data that students will use to complete the lessons and projects. A Readme file includes instructions for using the files. Adopters of this text are granted the right to install the Project Files on any stand-alone computer or network. The Project Files are available on the Instructor's Resource Kit CD-ROM, the Review Pack, and can also be downloaded from www.course.com.

SOLUTION FILES

Solution Files contain every file students are asked to create or modify in the lessons and projects. A Help file on the Instructor's Resource Kit includes information for using the Solution Files.

FIGURE FILES

Figure Files contain all the figures from the book in bitmap format. Use the figure files to create transparency masters or in a PowerPoint presentation.

SAM, SKILLS ASSESSMENT MANAGER FOR MICROSOFT OFFICE XP SAM^{xp}

SAM is the most powerful Office XP assessment and reporting tool that will help you gain a true understanding of your students' proficiency in Microsoft Word, Excel, Access, and PowerPoint 2002.

TOM, TRAINING ONLINE MANAGER FOR MICROSOFT OFFICE XP TOM

TOM is Course Technology's MOUS-approved training tool for Microsoft Office XP. Available via the World Wide Web and CD-ROM, TOM allows students to actively learn Office XP concepts and skills by delivering realistic practice through both guided and self-directed simulated instruction.

Certification Circle Series, SAM, and TOM: the true training and assessment solution for Office XP.

Contents

MOUS Microsoft Outlook 2002

CERTIFICATION CIRCLE™ *CORE*

Skill List

1. Start Outlook
2. Understand Outlook folders and items
3. Work with items and views
4. Get Help

Outlook 2002 is a powerful personal information manager and communication tool that is part of Microsoft Office XP. You can use Outlook to send and receive e-mail messages, schedule appointments, keep track of people, manage your to-do list, and much more. In this skill set, you become familiar with the basics of using Outlook. You will learn how to start and exit the program and how to view the different program components. You will copy the Project Files that accompany this book to the appropriate Outlook folders so that you will be able to complete the steps in the other skill sets. You will also learn how to view information in Outlook in different ways. Finally, you will learn how to access the Help system so that you can take full advantage of all the powerful tools and functionality that Outlook provides.

Getting Started

Start Outlook
Start and Exit Outlook

To start using the many useful features of Outlook, you need to start the program. Like any other Windows program, you can start Outlook using the Start menu on the taskbar. You can also start Outlook by double-clicking its program icon on the Windows desktop. If many people use Outlook on your computer, then you might need to enter a profile name in the Choose Profile dialog box before the Outlook program window opens. A **profile** is a group of e-mail accounts and address books set up for a particular user. Separate profiles are handy if you share your computer with others. By default, the Outlook setup program sets up only one profile on a computer. You close Outlook using the Exit command on the File menu.

Step 2
Your screen might look different than Figure GS-2, depending on how Outlook is set up on your computer.

Activity Steps

1. Click the **Start button** on the taskbar, then point to **Programs**
   See Figure GS-1.

2. Click **Microsoft Outlook** on the Programs menu (If you have profiles set up on your computer, then the Choose Profile dialog box will appear. Click the **Profile Name list arrow**, click your **Profile name**, enter your **password**, then click **OK**)
   The Outlook Program window opens.
   See Figure GS-2.

3. Click **File** on the menu bar, then click **Exit**

Figure GS-1: Programs menu

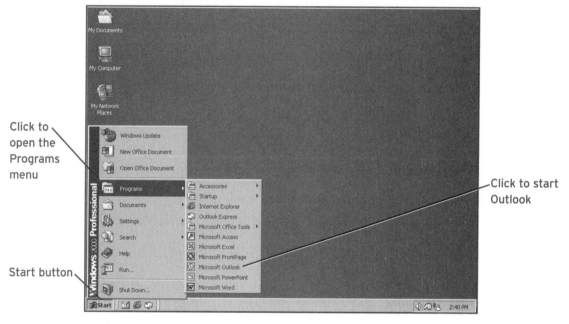

Click to open the Programs menu

Click to start Outlook

Start button

Figure GS-2: Outlook program window

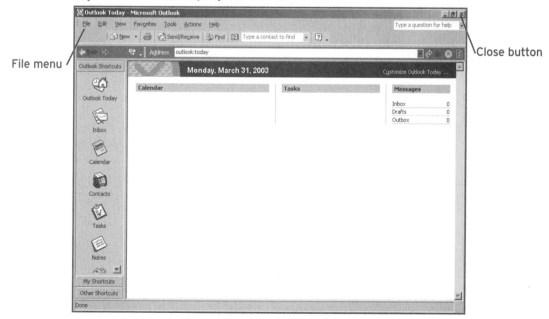

File menu

Close button

Getting Started

Getting Started with Outlook 2002

Understand Outlook Folders and Items

Switch Between Outlook Folders

Outlook is composed of several different **folders** that let you perform particular tasks and that store different kinds of information. The primary folders in Outlook are the **Inbox**, which you can use to send and receive e-mail, the **Calendar**, which you can use to manage your schedule, the **Contacts folder**, where you store information about people, such as their addresses and phone numbers, and the **Tasks folder**, where you keep track of your to-do list items. The **Outlook Today folder** shows you an at-a-glance view of items in your Calendar, Tasks, and Inbox folders. See Table GS-1 for a description of the other default Outlook folders. An **item** is a basic piece of information that is stored in an Outlook folder, such as an e-mail message or a Calendar appointment. To open a folder and view the items it contains, you click its icon on the **Outlook Bar**, located along the left edge of the Outlook window. The contents of the folder are displayed in the **View pane**, which is the large area to the right of the Outlook Bar. You can also open a folder by clicking its icon on the **Folder list**, which you can open using the View menu. The name of the open folder appears in the **Folder banner**, just above the Outlook Bar.

When you first start Outlook, the Outlook Bar displays the icons for the Outlook Shortcuts group. You can display other icons on the Outlook Bar by clicking My Shortcuts or Other Shortcuts on the Outlook Bar.

Activity Steps

1. Start **Outlook**, if necessary, choose your **Profile name**, type your **password**, then click **OK**
   The Outlook program window opens, and the View pane displays the contents of the current folder.

2. Click the **Calendar icon** 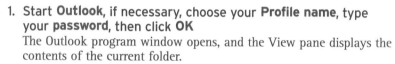 on the Outlook Bar
   The Calendar folder opens.
   See Figure GS-3.

3. Click **Calendar** in the Folder banner
   The Folder List opens.

4. Click the **push pin** in the upper-right corner of the Folder List to keep the Folder List open
   The Calendar resizes itself so that both the Calendar and the Folder List appear in the Outlook window.

5. Click the **Inbox folder** in the Folder List
   The Inbox folder opens, and the Folder List remains open. *See Figure GS-4.*

6. Click the **Folder List Close button**, then click **My Shortcuts** on the Outlook Bar
   The icons on the Outlook Bar change to show the icons for Drafts, Outbox, Sent Items, Journal, and Outlook Update.

Figure GS-3: Calendar folder open in Outlook window

Outlook Bar

Folder banner displays name of open folder

Calendar icon

View pane

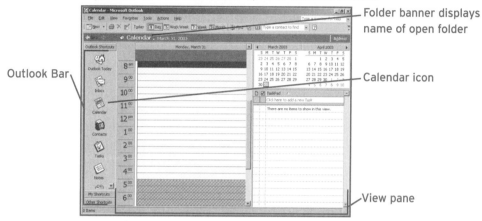

Figure GS-4: Inbox folder open with Folder List open

Folder List

Click to display icons for My Shortcuts group on the Outlook Bar

Click to display My Computer, My Documents, and Favorites icons on the Outlook Bar

Folder List Close button

Contents of Inbox folder (currently empty)

Inbox folder

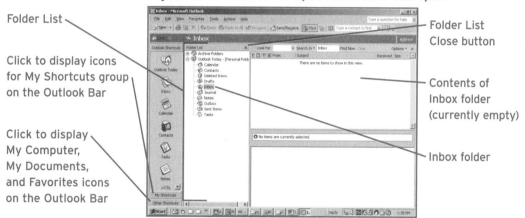

TABLE GS-1: Other Outlook folders and the type of information they store

folder	stores this type of information
Notes	Electronic "sticky notes" for recording thoughts, notes, ideas, and reminders
Journal	Log entries that describe completed tasks or events that have occurred
Drafts	In-progress e-mail messages
Outbox	Completed e-mail messages that have not yet been sent to the server for delivery to the recipients
Sent Items	E-mail messages that have been delivered to the recipients
Deleted Items	Items that have been removed using the Delete command
Outlook Update	Opens the Microsoft Office Web site where you can access resources, tools, and assistance

Use Toolbars, Menus, and Dialog Boxes

As in other Windows applications, you perform actions in Outlook using commands on menus or buttons on toolbars. The **menu bar** is located at the top of the Outlook window, just below the **title bar**. To execute a menu command, click a menu name on the menu bar to open the menu, then click a command on the open menu. When you first click a menu name on the menu bar, a short list of menu items opens. If you click the double arrows at the bottom of a menu, the **full menu** will open, displaying the complete list of commands for that menu. If more information is required to complete a command, a dialog box will open. A **dialog box** is a window from which you need to make selections or in which you need to type information in order for a task to be completed. You can also use toolbar buttons to perform actions. The **toolbar** is located directly above the Folder banner and contains buttons that you can click to perform tasks appropriate for the current folder. By default, the Standard toolbar is open. The toolbar buttons and menu commands that are available at any given time change depending on which folder is open.

Activity Steps

1. Click **Outlook Shortcuts** on the Outlook Bar, then click the **Calendar icon** 📇 on the Outlook Bar
The Calendar folder opens, showing time slots for today.

2. Click the **Week button** 7️⃣ Week on the toolbar
The Calendar format changes to show the days of the current week. Today's date is highlighted.

3. Click **View** on the menu bar
The short version of the View menu opens.
See Figure GS-5.

4. Click the **double arrows** at the bottom of the menu, if necessary
The full menu opens.

5. Point to **Go To** on the menu, then click **Go to Date** on the submenu that appears
The Go To Date dialog box appears.
See Figure GS-6.

6. Click the **Date list arrow** to open a small calendar for the current month, click the **date for tomorrow** on the calendar, then click **OK**
Tomorrow's date is highlighted on the Calendar.

7. Click **Today** on the toolbar, then click the **Day button** 1️⃣ Day on the toolbar
The Calendar now shows today's date in Day format.

You can reposition the toolbar by dragging it to a different location anywhere in the Outlook window.

Figure GS-5: View menu

Click to
display
full menu

Calendar
icon

Week button

Partial
View menu

Figure GS-6: Go To Date dialog box

Date list arrow

extra!

Displaying other toolbars

Outlook has three toolbars. By default, only the Standard toolbar is displayed. You might also want to display the Advanced toolbar, which contains buttons for performing additional Outlook tasks, or the Web toolbar, which contains buttons to help you view Web pages. To display the Advanced toolbar or the Web toolbar, point to the Standard toolbar, right-click, then click the name of the toolbar you want to display.

Getting Started

Getting Started with Outlook 2002

Work with Items and Views

Copy Calendar, Contacts, and Inbox Items to Outlook Folders

This book comes with a large number of Project Files, most of which are Outlook items that you will use for practice. In order to complete the steps in the remaining activities in this book, you need to copy the Project Files from Windows Explorer to the appropriate Outlook folder. For instance, to copy a Calendar item located in Windows Explorer to the Calendar folder, you drag the item from its folder in Windows Explorer over to the Calendar icon on the Outlook Bar. Before you begin the steps in this activity, make sure that you close all other applications so that only Outlook is running. You need to complete both this activity and the following one in order to copy all the files needed for the activities in this book.

Step 1
If you are using Microsoft Windows 98, click Start, click Programs, then click Windows Explorer.

Activity Steps

1. Click the **Start button**, point to **Programs**, point to **Accessories**, click **Windows Explorer**, then maximize the Windows Explorer window if necessary
Windows Explorer opens.

2. Locate and then click the **Outlook MOUS Cert Circle Project Files folder** in the Folders pane of Windows Explorer
Six folders appear in the right pane of Windows Explorer, along with three other files.
See Figure GS-7.

3. Right-click **the taskbar**, then click **Tile Windows Vertically** on the shortcut menu
The Outlook program window and the Windows Explorer window now appear side by side on your screen.

4. Double-click the **Calendar Items folder** in the right pane of the Windows Explorer window, click **Edit** on the Windows Explorer menu bar, then click **Select All**
See Figure GS-8.

5. Drag all the selected files to the **Calendar icon** on the Outlook Bar
The selected items are copied to your Calendar folder in Outlook.

6. Click the **Contacts Items folder** in the Folders pane of the Windows Explorer window, click **Edit** on the Windows Explorer menu bar, click **Select All**, then drag all the selected files to the **Contacts icon** on the Outlook Bar

7. Click the **Inbox Items folder** in the Folders pane of Windows Explorer, click **Edit** on the menu bar, click **Select All**, then drag the selected items to the **Inbox icon** on the Outlook Bar

Figure GS-7: Project Files in Windows Explorer

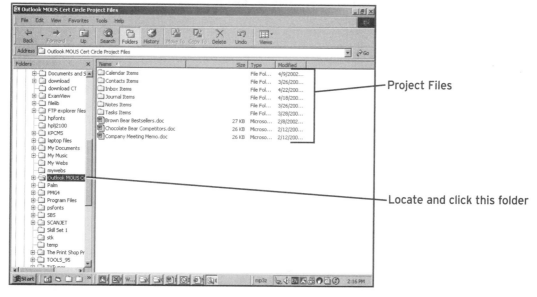

Project Files

Locate and click this folder

Figure GS-8: Windows Explorer and Outlook side by side

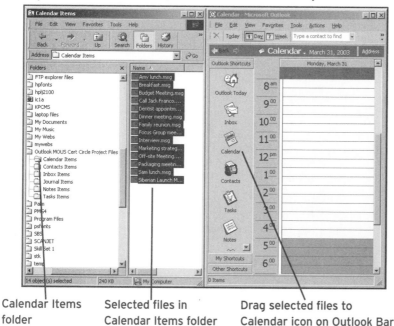

Calendar Items folder

Selected files in Calendar Items folder

Drag selected files to Calendar icon on Outlook Bar

extra!

Changing the default folder that opens when Outlook starts

When you first start Outlook, the Outlook Today folder opens by default. To specify that a different folder should open when Outlook starts, click Tools on the menu bar, click Options, click the Other tab, click Advanced Options, click the Startup in this folder list arrow, click a folder of your choice, then click OK twice.

Getting Started

Work with Items and Views

Copy Journal, Notes, and Tasks Items to Outlook Folders

This activity is a continuation of the previous activity, "Copy Calendar, Contacts, and Inbox Items to Outlook Folders." Make sure you complete the previous activity before starting this one. In the steps below, you will copy the Journal, Notes, and Tasks items from your Project Files folder to the appropriate Outlook folder.

You can use Outlook to browse for any file on your computer, network, or the Web. To do this, click Other Shortcuts on the Outlook Bar to display the My Computer, My Documents, and Favorites icons. Click any of these icons as appropriate to locate the file you want.

Activity Steps

1. Make sure that both Windows Explorer and Outlook are open on your screen, and that the **Outlook MOUS Cert Circle Project Files folder** is selected in the Folders pane of Windows Explorer

2. Click **My Shortcuts** on the Outlook Bar
   The icons in the Outlook Bar change.
   See Figure GS-9.

3. Click the **Journal Items folder** in the left pane of the Windows Explorer window, click **Edit** on the Windows Explorer menu bar, click **Select All**, then drag the **selected items** from the right pane of Windows Explorer to the **Journal icon** on the Outlook Bar
   The items are copied to your Journal folder in Outlook.

4. Click **Outlook Shortcuts** on the Outlook Bar
   The icons on the Outlook Bar change again.

5. Click the **Notes Items folder** in the left pane of the Windows Explorer window, click **Edit** on the Windows Explorer menu bar, then click **Select All**
   See Figure GS-10.

6. Drag the selected items to the **Notes icon** on the Outlook Bar

7. Click the **Tasks Items folder** in the left pane of Windows Explorer, then drag the **Write monthly status report.msg** item from the right pane of Windows Explorer to the **Tasks icon** on the Outlook Bar
   All the Project Files are now copied to the appropriate Outlook folders.

8. Click **File** on the Windows Explorer menu bar, click **Close**, then click the **Maximize button** on the Outlook window

Figure GS-9: Outlook Bar with My Shortcuts icons displayed

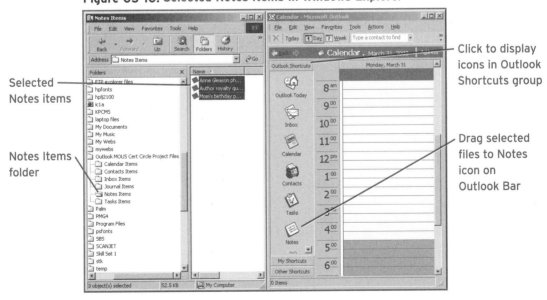

Journal icon

Journal Items folder

My Shortcuts icon group button

Icons in My Shortcuts icon group

Figure GS-10: Selected Notes items in Windows Explorer

Selected Notes items

Notes Items folder

Click to display icons in Outlook Shortcuts group

Drag selected files to Notes icon on Outlook Bar

Getting Started

Work with Items and Views

Understand Views

A **view** is a particular way to display the items in an Outlook folder. When you click a folder icon on the Outlook Bar, the items contained in that folder appear in the default view for that folder. Each folder has many different views available so that you can see the same information in different ways. For instance, the default view for the Calendar folder is Day/Week/Month view, which shows your appointments for the current day. You might want to change this view to show only active appointments, so that you can see all of your active appointments in a table. You can change a view by choosing a view type on the Current View menu. The available views for each folder are unique to that folder; however, the method for changing views is the same no matter what folder you are using.

Step 3
Your active appointments might be different from the ones shown in figure GS-12, depending on the date you complete these steps.

Activity Steps

1. Click the **Calendar icon** [icon], if necessary, on the Outlook Bar

2. Click **View** on the menu bar, then point to **Current View**
   A list of available views appears on the Current View menu.
   See Figure GS-11.

3. Click **Active Appointments**
   All your active appointments appear in table format.
   See Figure GS-12.

4. Click **View** on the menu bar, point to **Current View**, then click **Day/Week/Month**
   The default view is restored.

Figure GS-11: Current View menu

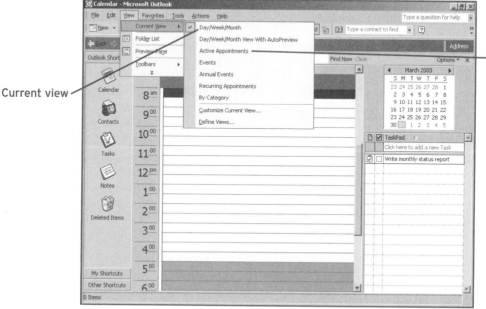

Current view

Click to display appointments in table format

Figure GS-12: Calendar in Active Appointments view

Subject column heading

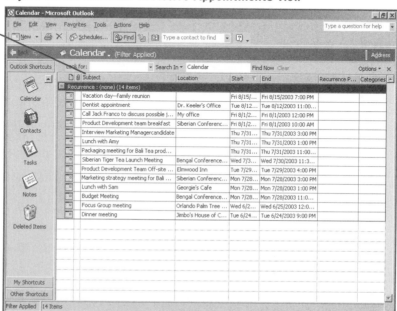

Get Help

Access the Help System

Outlook is a powerful program packed with an impressive array of features. As you use Outlook you will probably need help completing certain tasks and will probably also have questions about how to take full advantage of all of its functionality. Fortunately, like all the other applications in Microsoft Office XP, Outlook comes with a powerful Help system. There are many ways to access Help. You can type a question or keywords in the **Ask a Question box**, located at the right end of the menu bar. Once you enter a question or keywords, the Ask a Question box presents a list of related topics. Clicking a topic opens the Microsoft Outlook Help window, where you can view additional topics and perform additional topic searches, using one of three tabs. The **Contents tab** shows a comprehensive listing of all the Help topics available. The **Answer Wizard tab** lets you type a question or keywords in a box and then search for related topics. The **Index tab** lets you search for topics that contain particular keywords. Some of the topics listed in the Help window are actually stored on the Web. Clicking one of these topics will open the relevant Web page on the Microsoft Web site.

Activity Steps

1. Click in the Ask a Question box, type **How do I hide a toolbar?**, then press **[Enter]**
   A list of Help topics related to the question appears.
   See Figure GS-13.

2. Click **Show or hide a toolbar**
   The Microsoft Outlook Help window opens, with the topic you selected in the right pane.
   See Figure GS-14.

Step 4
You can resize the panes in the Help window by dragging the split bar that divides the two panes.

3. Click **Show All** in the upper-right corner of the Help window, then read all the text in the right pane of the Help window

4. Click the **Contents tab** in the left pane of the Help window, click the **(+)** next to Getting Started with Microsoft Office, then click the **(+)** next to Getting Help

5. Click **About getting help while you work**, click **Show All** in the right pane, then read the topic in the right pane

6. Click the **Index tab**, type **toolbar** in the Type keywords box, click **Search**, then view the list of topics that appears below **3 Choose a topic**

7. Click the **Answer Wizard tab**, type **change views**, then click **Search**

8. View the topics that appear, then click the **Microsoft Outlook Help Close button**

Figure GS-13: Ask a Question box topics

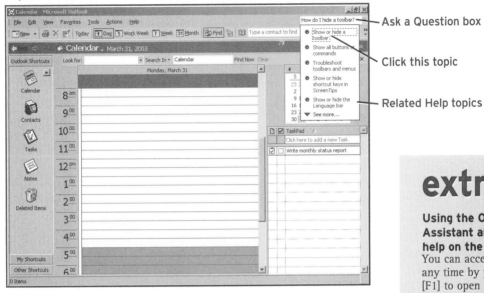

Ask a Question box

Click this topic

Related Help topics

Figure GS-14: Microsoft Outlook Help window

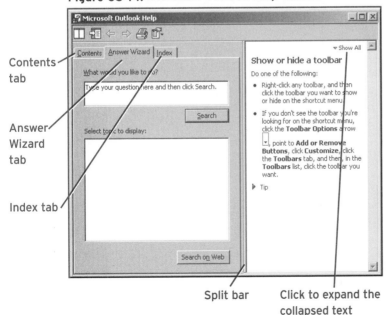

Contents tab

Answer Wizard tab

Index tab

Split bar

Click to expand the collapsed text

extra!

Using the Office Assistant and getting help on the Web

You can access Help at any time by pressing [F1] to open the Office Assistant, an animated character that lets you type a search word or question in its yellow bubble to get help. The Office Assistant also appears as you work to offer context-sensitive help. You can hide the Office Assistant by clicking Help on the menu bar, then clicking Hide the Office Assistant or right-clicking the Office Assistant and choosing Hide from the shortcut menu. You can also get help and find valuable technical resources on the Microsoft Office Web site, which you can access directly from Outlook. To do this, click Help on the menu bar, then click Office on the Web.

Getting Started

Getting Started with Outlook 2002

Target Your Skills

1 Use Figure GS-15 as a guide. Start Outlook, open the Calendar folder, then use the Month button on the toolbar to make your screen look like the figure. Open the Folder List as shown. Change the view to Active Appointments view, then close the Folder List. Open each folder on the Outlook Bar and notice the Project Files that you copied. Exit Outlook.

2 Use Help to display the topic shown in Figure GS-16. Locate the topic shown by typing appropriate keywords in the Ask a Question box. Once you locate the topic shown, follow the on-screen instructions to take a tour of Outlook. Then use the Index tab of the Help window to learn how to add a new user profile to Outlook. Finally, use the Contents tab to learn about the new features of Outlook 2002, then use the Answer Wizard to learn how to hide the Outlook Bar.

Figure GS-15

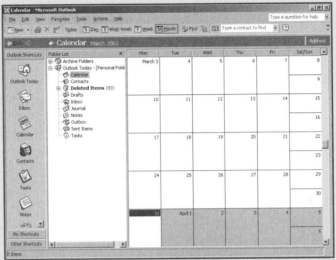

Figure GS-16

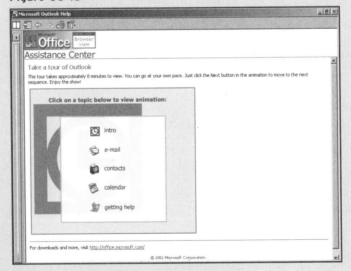

Skill List

1. Display and print messages
2. Compose and send messages
3. Insert signatures and attachments
4. Customize views

You can use Outlook to send and receive electronic messages, or **e-mail**, over a network or the Internet. In this skill set, you will learn how to open and print a message you receive, and also how to reply to, forward, compose, and send messages. You will also learn how to add personalized information, called a **signature**, to the end of a message. Finally, you will learn how to view, group, and sort the items in your Inbox in various ways to make it easier to find and manage messages.

Skill Set 1

Creating and Viewing Messages

Display and Print Messages

View a Message

To view your e-mail messages in Outlook, you need to open the Inbox folder. When you open the Inbox folder, a list of your messages appears in the order you received them, with the most recent messages listed first. Unread messages appear in bold, marked with a closed envelope icon. Below the list of messages is the **Preview pane**. When you click a message header in the Inbox, the text of the message appears in the Preview pane. If a message is short, you can view all of it in the Preview pane without scrolling. If it is long, you can open it in its own window, called the **Message form**. You open and close the Preview pane using the Preview Pane command on the View menu. If you need to find a particular message in your Inbox, but don't want to click each message individually to view it in the Preview pane, you can use the **AutoPreview** feature to display the first three lines of each message in the Inbox.

Steps 3 and 5
If you have trouble locating the messages in Steps 3 or 5, click the From column heading to sort the messages by the name of the sender, then scroll to locate the messages from Linda Miller or Muriel Baldwin.

Activity Steps

1. Start **Outlook**, then if necessary, choose your **Profile name**, click **OK**, type your **password**, then click **OK**

2. Click the **Inbox icon** on the Outlook bar, if necessary, to view the contents of your Inbox folder

3. Scroll up or down in your Inbox to locate the **Meeting attendees message** from Linda Miller, then click this message to view it in the Preview pane
   See Figure 1-1.

4. Click **View** on the menu bar, then click **Preview Pane**
   The Preview pane closes, and you can see more of your messages.

5. Double-click the **Summer reunion message** from Muriel Baldwin to open the Message form
   See Figure 1-2.

6. Read the message, click the **Message form Close button**, click **View** on the menu bar, then click **AutoPreview**
   The first three lines of each message now appear under each message heading.

7. Click **View** on the menu bar, click **AutoPreview**, click **View** on the menu bar, then click **Preview Pane**
   AutoPreview is now turned off, and the Preview pane is open at the bottom of your screen.

Skill 1

Display and Print Messages

Figure 1-1: Selected message open in Preview pane

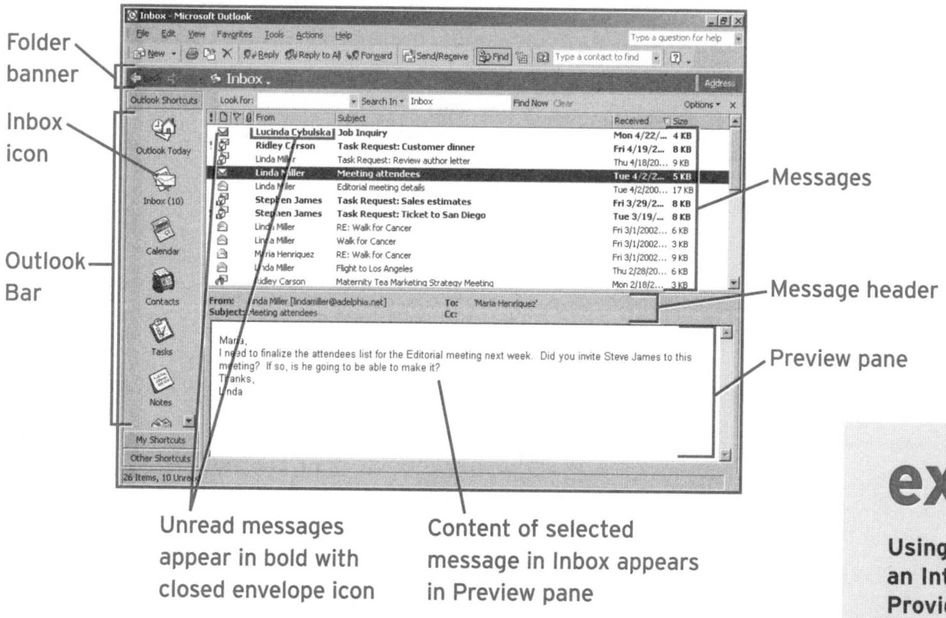

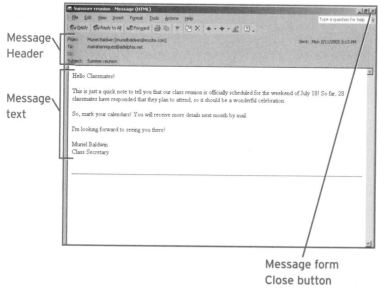

Folder banner
Inbox icon
Outlook Bar
Messages
Message header
Preview pane
Unread messages appear in bold with closed envelope icon
Content of selected message in Inbox appears in Preview pane

Figure 1-2: Open message in Message form

Message Header
Message text
Message form Close button

extra!

Using Outlook with an Internet Service Provider

If you are using an Internet Service Provider with Outlook, then you will see a Send/Receive button on your toolbar. Clicking this button transfers any new messages that you have received from the server to your Inbox. Therefore, if you are using an Internet Service Provider, you must click the Send/Receive button to check for new e-mail messages. The figures in this book show the Send/Receive button. If you are using Outlook on a corporate network, any new messages you receive will automatically be transferred to your Inbox from the server.

Skill Set 1

Creating and Viewing Messages

Display and Print Messages

Open an Attachment

Though you can include a lot of information in an e-mail message, sometimes it's more efficient to send a brief message and attach a file with additional information. For example, a colleague might attach an Excel spreadsheet to a message about your department's budget. To open and view an attachment, you must have the software in which the attachment was created, or else have another software program that is able to open the file. Messages that have attachments appear with a paper clip icon next to them in the Inbox. You can open an attachment either from the Preview pane or from the Message form. You can choose to save an attachment to a folder on a disk, or you can open an attachment without saving it first. To avoid harming your computer, never open or save an attachment unless you are completely confident that the file is free of viruses.

To open an attachment from the Preview pane, double-click the attachment filename in the Preview pane message header.

Activity Steps

1. Click the **Inbox icon** 🔲 on the Outlook Bar, if necessary

2. Double-click the **Company meeting message** from Linda Miller (you might have to scroll to locate it)

3. In the message header, right-click the filename **Company Meeting Memo.doc**, then click **Open**
   The Opening Mail Attachment dialog box opens.
   See Figure 1-3.

4. Click the **Open it option button**, then click **OK** (if a dialog box opens asking if you want to merge changes, click **No**)
   A document opens in the Word program window.
   See Figure 1-4.

5. Read the memo, click **File** on the menu bar, then click **Exit**
   The Word program window closes and you return to the Outlook window.

6. Click the **Message form Close button**

Figure 1-3: Opening Mail Attachment dialog box

Click to open the attached file from its current location

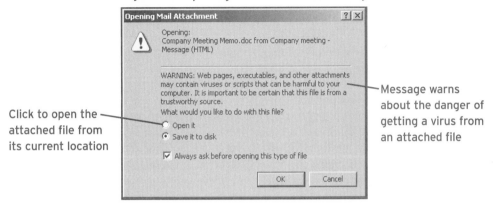

Message warns about the danger of getting a virus from an attached file

Figure 1-4: Attachment opened in Word program window

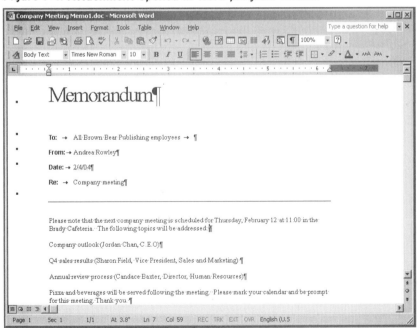

Skill Set 1

Creating and Viewing Messages

Display and Print Messages
Print a Message

If a message is particularly long or contains important information, you might decide to print it so that you have a hard copy to file or read. You can print an e-mail message with the default settings using the Print button on the Standard toolbar. However, you can make changes to the default print settings using the Page Setup and Print dialog boxes. The Page Setup dialog box lets you choose the orientation of the paper, change margin settings, or add a customized header or footer. A **header** is specified text that prints at the top of every page, and a **footer** is specified text that prints at the bottom of every page. You can use the Print dialog box to change other settings, such as which printer to use, how many copies to print, whether to print with a wide (**landscape**) or tall (**portrait**) orientation, or whether to print the message in color or in black and white. You can also specify to use fewer pages to print an e-mail message that is several pages long.

If you don't have Windows 2000 installed, you might not see the Print dialog box shown in Figure 1-6. If this is the case, skip steps 4, 5, and 6 and click the Print button on the Message toolbar to print the message with the current print settings.

Activity Steps

1. Click the **Inbox icon** 📧, if necessary, then double-click the **Editorial meeting details message** from Linda Miller

2. Click **File** on the menu bar, point to **Page Setup**, then click **Memo Style**
   The Page Setup dialog box opens.
   See Figure 1-5.

3. Select the text in the Left margin box, type 1, select the text in the Right margin box, type 1, then click **OK**

4. Click **File** on the menu bar, click **Print**, then click the **Layout tab**
   See Figure 1-6.

5. Click the **Pages Per Sheet list arrow**, then click **2**

6. Click **Print**
   The two pages of the message print on one page.

7. Close the **Editorial meeting details Message form**

Figure 1-5: Page Setup dialog box

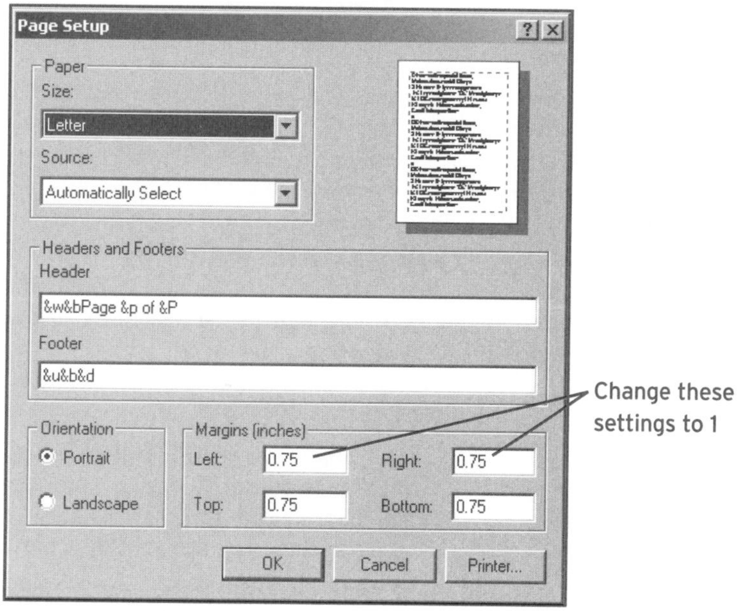

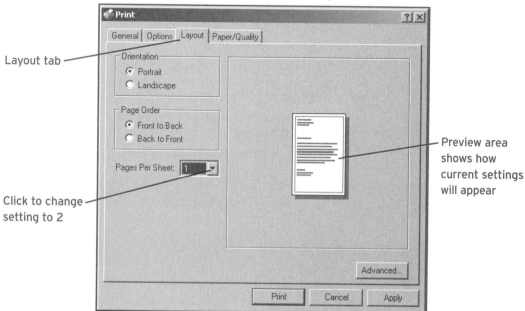

Change these settings to 1

Figure 1-6: Layout tab of the Print dialog box

Layout tab

Preview area shows how current settings will appear

Click to change setting to 2

Skill Set 1
Creating and Viewing Messages

Compose and Send Messages
Reply to a Message

One of the most common e-mail tasks is responding to messages sent to you by others. You can use the Reply button to reply to only the sender, or you can use the Reply to All button to address your response to everyone who received the message. When you click the Reply or Reply to All button, a new Message form opens that is automatically addressed to the sender. If you use the Reply to All button, the sender is listed in the To: box and all recipients of the original message are listed in the Cc: box. The insertion point is in the message body, ready for you to start typing your message. If you have Microsoft Word 2002 installed on your computer, the message form will actually open in Word, providing you with a powerful array of tools to use to format and edit your message. By default, Outlook uses Word as its editor.

You can also use keyboard shortcuts to reply to messages. To reply only to the sender, press [Ctrl][R]. To reply to all recipients of the original message, press [Ctrl][Shift][R].

Activity Steps

1. Click the **Inbox icon** 📥, if necessary, then click the **From column heading**

   The messages are sorted by sender in alphabetical order, making it easier to find messages sent by a particular sender.

2. Double-click the **Job Inquiry message** from Lucinda Cybulska

   See Figure 1-7.

3. Read the message, then click the **Reply button** on the toolbar

   The Reply form opens. The insertion point is already in the message box, above the text of the Job Inquiry message.

4. Type the following text:

   Thanks for your message. I would be happy to meet with you on June 18 at 10:00 in my office. Please contact my assistant, Linda Miller, if you need directions.

5. Compare your screen with Figure 1-8, then click **Send** on the Message toolbar

6. Click the **Job Inquiry Message form Close button**, then click the **Received column heading** in the Inbox to sort the messages by date

Figure 1-7: Open message in Message form

Click to reply to the sender only and not other recipients of the original message

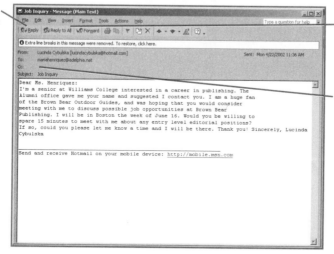

Click to reply to the sender and all recipients of the original message

Cc: line shows no other recipients

Figure 1-8: Completed message in Reply form

Original sender automatically appears in To: box

Type reply text here

Original message automatically appears in message body

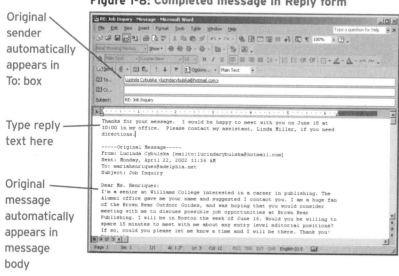

extra!

Using the Send/Receive button

If you are using Outlook on a corporate network, then clicking the Send button in the Message form automatically transfers your reply or new message to the server so it can be delivered to your recipient. However, if you are using Outlook with an Internet Service Provider, and if you are working off-line, then clicking Send in the Message form only transfers your message to your Outbox folder. In order to transfer your message from your Outbox folder to the ISP's server, you must click the Send/Receive button on the Standard toolbar in the Outlook window.

Skill Set 1

Creating and Viewing Messages

Compose and Send Messages

Forward a Message

If you receive a message that is important for others to read, you can forward the message to them using the Forward button on the toolbar. When you click the Forward button, a Message form opens, with the insertion point in the To: box and a copy of the message displayed in the message body. In the To: box, type the addresses of the people to whom you want to forward the message. You can type additional text above the message to explain why you are forwarding it, or you can forward the message by itself. If Word is installed on your computer, the Message form will open in Microsoft Word, the default editor for Outlook.

You can also forward a message by clicking Actions on the menu bar, then clicking Forward, or by pressing [Ctrl][F].

Activity Steps

1. Click the **Inbox icon** 🗂, then click the **Reunion attendees message** from Muriel Baldwin

2. Click the **Forward button** on the Standard toolbar
   The Message form opens, with the insertion point in the To: box.

3. Type your e-mail address

4. Click at the top of the message area, then type **FYI**
   See Figure 1-9.

5. Click **Send** on the Message toolbar

6. If you are using Outlook with an Internet Service Provider, click the **Send/Receive button** on the Message toolbar, wait a minute or two, then click the **Send/Receive button** again (If you are using Outlook on a corporate network, skip to Step 7)
   The message that you forwarded appears in the Inbox, with the letters FW preceding the Subject title.
   See Figure 1-10.

7. Click the **FW: Reunion attendees message**, then press **[Delete]**

Figure 1-9: Forward Message form with To: address and text added

Type your e-mail address here

Type additional text here

Forwarded message appears here automatically

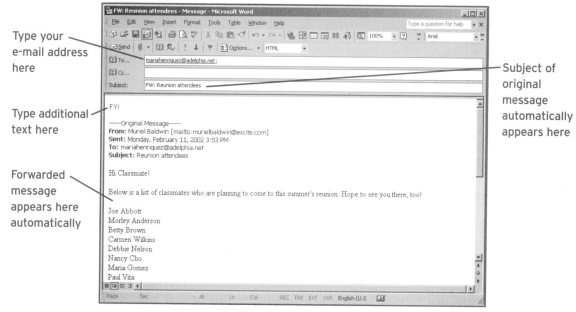

Subject of original message automatically appears here

Figure 1-10: Inbox with new forwarded message

Your e-mail address will appear here

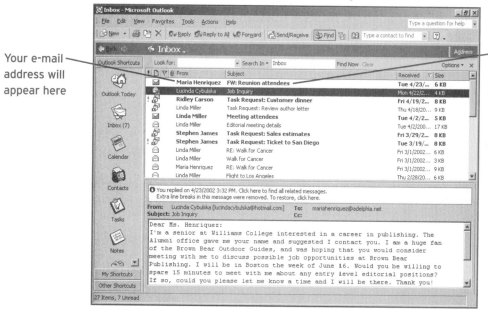

Forwarded message in Inbox

Skill Set 1

Creating and Viewing Messages

Compose and Send Messages
Create a New Mail Message

You can create new messages in Outlook and send them to recipients who are part of your corporate work group, or to recipients with an Internet e-mail address. When you create a new e-mail message, a new Message form opens. If Microsoft Word 2002 was installed on your computer at the same time as Outlook, then your Message form will open in Microsoft Word, providing you with a powerful array of formatting and editing tools to make your message more visually compelling. Otherwise, Outlook will be your editor. No matter which editor you have, you complete the message header in the same way. You first type the addresses of the recipients in the To: and Cc: boxes, then type a title for your message in the Subject box. You then type your message into the message body, then use the Send button to place the message in your Outbox. If you are using an Internet Service Provider, you need to use the Send/Receive button on the Standard toolbar to transmit the message from the Outbox folder to your mail server.

If Word is not currently your editor and you would like it to be, click Tools on the menu bar, click Options to open the Options dialog box, click the Mail Format tab, then click the Use Microsoft Word to edit e-mail messages check box, then click OK.

Activity Steps

1. Click the **Inbox icon,** , if necessary, then click the **New Mail Message button** New on the Standard toolbar

2. Type **lucindacybulska@hotmail.com**, then click in the **Cc: box**

3. Type your e-mail address, then press **[Tab]** twice to move the insertion point to the Subject box

4. Type **June 18 meeting**, then press **[Tab]** to move the insertion point to the message body

5. Type **I need to change the time of our meeting on June 18 to 11:00. Please let me know if this is a problem for you. Thanks.** *See Figure 1-11.*

6. Click **Send** on the Message toolbar, then if you are using an Internet Service Provider, click **Send/Receive** on the Standard toolbar as needed until the message appears in your Inbox
   Depending on the speed of your mail server, the new message should appear in your Inbox.

7. Click the **June 18 meeting message**, read the message in the Preview pane, then click the **Delete button** on the Standard toolbar
   The message is deleted.

Figure 1-11: Completed message in Message form

Click to place message in Outbox folder

Type your e-mail address here

Message body

Type meaningful subject for your message here

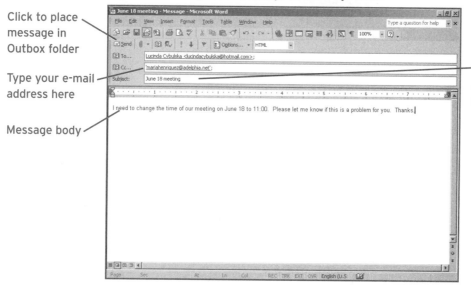

extra!

Creating a new Office document from within Outlook

You can create a new Word document, Excel worksheet, or PowerPoint presentation from within Outlook. To do this, click the New list arrow on the Standard toolbar, then click Office Document. The New Office Document dialog box opens, as shown in Figure 1-12. Click the program icon you want to use, then click OK. The program opens. To return to Outlook, click the Outlook program icon on the taskbar.

Figure 1-12: New Office Document dialog box

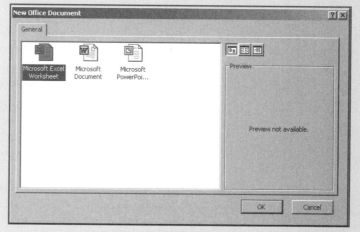

Skill Set 1

Creating and Viewing Messages

Compose and Send Messages
Use the Address Book

If you exchange frequent e-mails with particular people, you might want to store their e-mail addresses and other information in the Address Book to save time and ensure accuracy. The **Address Book** stores names, addresses, phone numbers, and other information about people you know. Entries in the Address Book are called **contacts**, and are stored in the Contacts folder in Outlook. You enter each new e-mail address and other information, such as address and phone number, in the **Contact form**. To access e-mail addresses for all the contacts in your Contacts folder, click the To: button in the message header and choose the recipients.

Unless you specify otherwise, the full name and e-mail address of each contact will appear in the message header when you select it from the Select Names dialog box. You can control how the name of the contact appears by entering the name precisely as you want it to appear in the Display as box in the Contact form.

Activity Steps

1. Click the **Inbox icon** , click **Tools** on the menu bar, then click **Address Book**
The Address Book dialog box opens.

2. Verify that **Contacts** is selected in the Show Names from the box, then click the **New Entry button** on the toolbar

3. In the New Entry dialog box, verify that **New Contact** is selected, then click **OK**
The Contact form opens.

4. Maximize the Contact form, if necessary, type **Muriel Baldwin** in the Full Name box, click in the E-mail box, then type **murielbaldwin@excite.com**
See Figure 1-13. Notice that Baldwin, Muriel automatically appeared in the File as box when you clicked in the E-mail box.

5. Click the **Save and Close button** on the toolbar, then click the **Close button** in the Address Book dialog box

6. Click the **New Mail Message button** on the toolbar to open the Message form, then click the **Address book button** to the left of the To: box
The Select Names dialog box opens. Muriel Baldwin now appears in the Name list. *See Figure 1-14.*

7. Click **Muriel Baldwin** in the Name list, click the **To button**, click **OK**, click in the Subject box, type **Reunion**, press **[Tab]**, type **I plan to attend this summer's reunion.**, then click the **Send button**

Figure 1-13: Contact form

Save and Close button

Automatically entered; based on Full Name box contents

Type contact's e-mail address here

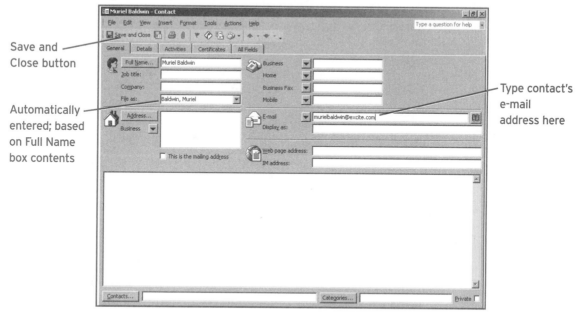

Figure 1-14: Select Names dialog box with new name

Your list of names might be different

To button

Muriel Baldwin appears in the list

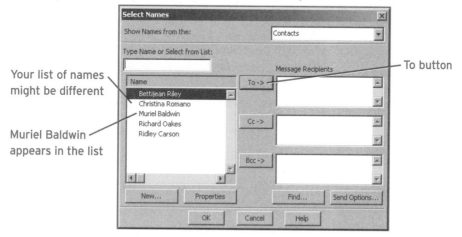

Skill Set 1
Creating and Viewing Messages

Insert Signatures and Attachments
Insert and Remove Signatures

If you want the same information to appear at the end of all your messages, you can save time by inserting a signature. A **signature** is a block of text that you can specify to appear at the end of a message. Usually a signature includes your name, job, title, address, and phone number, although you can create signatures that include anything you want, such as a motto or favorite saying. You can create several different signatures and choose an appropriate one for a specific message. To create a new signature, you use the Signatures command on the Mail Format tab of the Options dialog box. You can apply formatting to signatures using any of the formatting or special effects tools available with Word. Once you create a new signature, it will be inserted automatically at the end of your new messages. You can choose a different signature or specify that no signature appear by adjusting the settings in the Signature section of the Mail Format tab of the Options dialog box.

Activity Steps

1. Click the **Inbox icon** 🖼️, click **Tools** on the menu bar, click **Options**, then click the **Mail Format tab**

2. Click **Signatures** (to the bottom right of the dialog box), then click **New** in the Create Signature dialog box

3. Type **Maria Henriquez** in the Enter a name for your new signature box, verify that the **Start with a blank signature option button** is selected, then click **Next**

4. In the Edit Signature dialog box, type **Best wishes**, press **[Enter]**, type **Maria Henriquez**, press **[Enter]**, type **Editorial Director**, press **[Enter]**, then type **Brown Bear Publishing**
   See Figure 1-15.

5. Click **Finish**, then click **OK**
   The Mail Format tab of the Options dialog box appears. Notice that Maria Henriquez now appears in the Signature for new messages list box. *See Figure 1-16.*

6. Click **OK**, then click the **New Mail Message button** 📧 New ▾ on the toolbar
   The Message form opens. The Maria Henriquez signature appears in the message body.

7. Click the **Message form close button**, click the **Outlook program button** on the taskbar, click **Tools** on the menu bar, click **Options**, click the **Mail Format tab**, click **Signatures**, verify that the **Maria Henriquez signature** is selected, click **Remove**, click **Yes**, then click **OK** twice

Figure 1-15: Edit Signature dialog box

Use these buttons to format the text of a signature

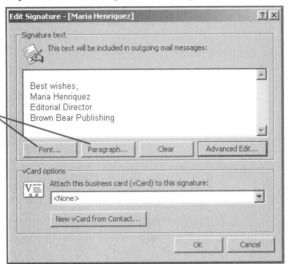

Figure 1-16: Mail Format tab of the Options dialog box

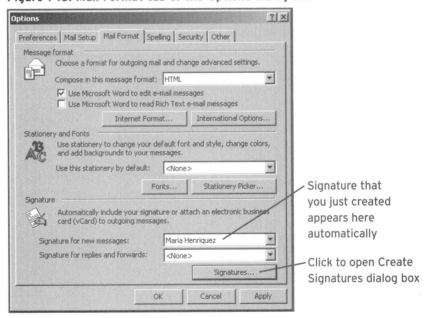

Signature that you just created appears here automatically

Click to open Create Signatures dialog box

Skill Set 1

Creating and Viewing Messages

Insert Signatures and Attachments

Insert Message Attachments

Though you can include a lot of information in an e-mail message, sometimes it is more efficient to send a message with a file attached to it. For instance, rather than writing a message that summarizes the contents of a memo, you could simply attach the memo file to the message so that the recipients can view it for themselves. You can attach any kind of file you want to an e-mail message; however, keep in mind that the recipient must have the appropriate software to view the file. You attach a file using the Insert File button on the Message form toolbar.

Step 8
If you are using Outlook with an Internet Service Provider, you also need to click the Send/Receive button on the toolbar to upload your message to the server. Your message will remain in your Outbox folder until you click Send/Receive on the toolbar.

Activity Steps

1. Click the **Inbox icon** 📥, then click the **New Mail Message button** 📧 New ▾ on the Standard toolbar

2. Type **lindamiller@adelphia.net** in the To: box, then click in the **Subject box**

3. Type **Bestseller list** in the Subject box, then press **[Tab]**

4. Type **Please make 25 copies of the attached bestseller list for the Editorial meeting. Thanks.**

5. Click the **Insert File button** 📎 ▾ on the Message toolbar

6. Navigate to the folder where your Project files are stored, then click **Brown Bear Bestsellers** in the file list
See Figure 1-17.

7. Click **Insert**
See Figure 1-18.

8. Click **Send** on the toolbar

Figure 1-17: Insert File dialog box

Your files might be located in a different folder

Your file list might be different

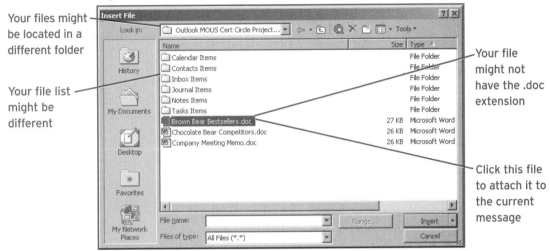

Your file might not have the .doc extension

Click this file to attach it to the current message

Figure 1-18: Message with file attachment

Click to send message

Attachment icon indicates type of file, Word in this case

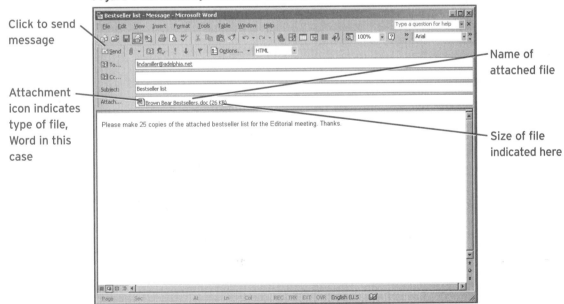

Name of attached file

Size of file indicated here

Skill Set 1

Creating and Viewing Messages

Customize Views
Changing Outlook Views

If you use e-mail frequently, and regularly receive a large number of messages, it can sometimes be difficult to locate a particular message. You can view your Outlook folders in a variety of ways to make it easy to locate particular messages or items. First, open the folder you want to view by clicking the down arrow next to the folder name in the Folder banner, then click the name of the folder you want to open. You can then use the commands on the Current View submenu to change how the information is displayed in the Outlook window. For instance, you can choose to group your messages by sender, or to show only unread messages.

You can sort the contents of any folder by clicking a gray column header. For instance, to sort the messages in your Inbox by sender in ascending alphabetical order, click the From gray header box at the top of the column. Click it again to sort in descending order.

Activity Steps

1. **Click View on the menu bar, point to Current View, then click By Sender**
   The messages in the Inbox are no longer visible; instead you see a list of headings of each sender's name, with a plus sign (+) next to each one.
   See Figure 1-19.

2. **Click the + sign next to Linda Miller**
   Ten messages appear under the From: Linda Miller heading.

3. **Click the down arrow next to Inbox in the Folder banner, then click Sent Items**
   Sent Items now appears in the Folder banner, indicating that this folder is open. A list of all the messages you have sent appears below.

4. **Click the Inbox icon [icon] on the Outlook Bar, click View on the menu bar, point to Current View, then click Unread Messages**
   Notice that (Filter Applied) appears in the Folder banner, indicating that some of the messages in this folder might not be showing. (In this case, the messages you have already read are not showing.)
   See Figure 1-20.

5. **Click View on the menu bar, point to Current View, then click Messages**

Figure 1-19: Inbox with messages grouped by Sender

Click plus sign to view messages from that sender

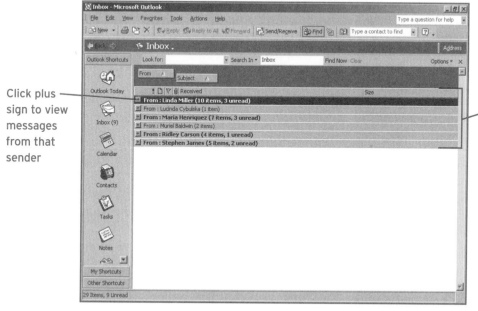

Messages are grouped by sender

Figure 1-20: Inbox with Unread Messages filter applied

Folder banner

Current folder name appears in Folder banner

Unread messages in Inbox folder (you might have a different number)

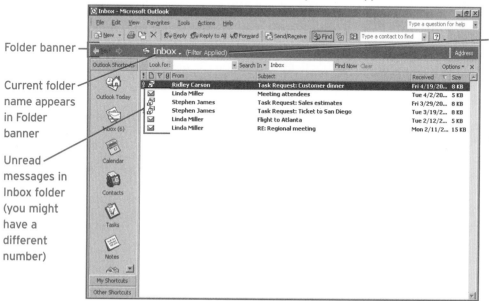

Indicates that filter is applied and some messages in open folder might not appear

Skill Set 1
Creating and Viewing Messages

Customize Views
Customize Outlook Views

You can customize the way the information in Outlook appears on your screen. For instance, you can change the way messages appear in your Inbox. By default, the Inbox shows fields for your messages that indicate the sender, the date you received the message, the size of the message, and the Subject. It also includes fields that convey other information, such as the importance of each message, or whether or not the message has an attachment. You can hide any of these fields, change their order, or add new fields using the Customize Views dialog box. You can also use this dialog box to specify that messages be grouped or sorted in a certain way, or to apply a filter to show only messages that contain certain information, such as the word "reunion" in the Subject field. Finally, you can change the way fonts appear for various parts of the Outlook window, and specify whether to include gridlines in the message header list. If you create a customized view and decide you prefer the original settings, you can use the Reset button in the Define Views dialog box to restore the defaults.

Step 4
You can also change the order of fields in the Show these fields in this order list by dragging them to a different position.

Activity Steps

1. Click **View** on the menu bar, point to **Current View**, then click **Customize Current View**
   The View Summary dialog box opens.
   See Figure 1-21.

2. Click **Fields**

3. Click **Cc** in the Available fields list, then click **Add**

4. With the Cc field selected, click **Move Up** three times to move the Cc field to just below the From field, then click **OK**

5. Click **Other Settings** in the View Summary dialog box, click the **Grid line style list arrow**, click **Dashes**, click the **Grid line color list arrow**, scroll up, click the **red rectangle**, then click **OK** twice
   See Figure 1-22.

6. Click **View** on the menu bar, point to **Current View**, click **Define Views**, click **Reset**, click **OK** in the dialog box that appears, then click **Close**
   The Inbox appears with its default view settings.

Figure 1-21: View Summary dialog box

Click to change the way fields are ordered on screen in current view

Click to enhance or change the appearance of elements in the current view

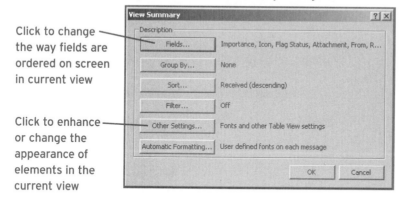

Figure 1-22: Inbox with dashed grid lines

Cc field now appears in this view, after the From field

Colored gridlines now appear

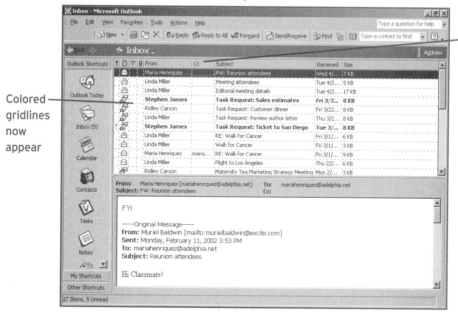

Skill Set 1

Creating and Viewing Messages

Target Your Skills

1 Use Figure 1-23 as a guide. Create three messages to yourself with the subject headings shown. Write the message text shown for the Travel schedule message; make up text for the other two messages. Use the Customize current View dialog box to change the fields so that they appear as shown. Add a blue gridline with the large dots style.

Figure 1-23

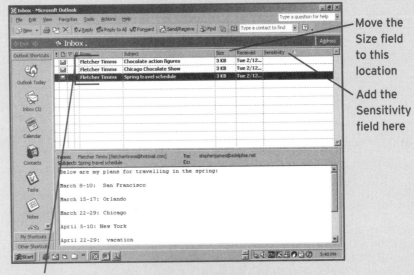

Move the Size field to this location

Add the Sensitivity field here

Your e-mail address should appear here

2 Use Figure 1-24 as a guide. Create the message shown, and attach the Project File Chocolate Bear Competitors. Create a new signature named Sugar Bear Productions with the text shown in the figure. (Include the text from "Regards" to the end of the message in the signature.) Send the message to yourself, then view the message and the attachment.

Figure 1-24

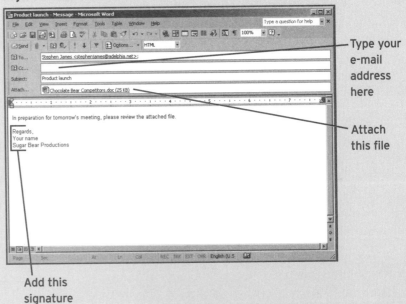

Type your e-mail address here

Attach this file

Add this signature

Skill List

1. Add appointments, meetings, and events to the Calendar
2. Apply conditional formats to the Outlook Calendar
3. Respond to meeting requests
4. Use categories to manage appointments
5. Print Calendars

Managing your time can be a huge challenge, but fortunately, the Calendar in Outlook has powerful tools that can help. In this skill set, you will learn to use the Calendar to manage your schedule by adding single appointments, as well as appointments that recur at regular intervals, to your Calendar. You will learn ways to apply color-coded labels to your appointments so you can quickly identify the type of appointments you have scheduled. You will learn how to categorize appointments so you can view related appointments together. You will also learn how to use the Calendar to schedule meetings and invite participants, as well how to respond to meeting requests sent by others. Finally, you'll learn how to print your Calendar in a format that works best for a particular circumstance.

Skill Set 2

Scheduling

Add Appointments, Meetings, and Events to the Calendar

Add Appointments to the Calendar

You can use the Calendar in Outlook to manage your schedule just like you would a paper-based date book, by entering appointments for particular dates and times. In Outlook, an **appointment** is an activity, such as a meeting, that takes place on a specific day at a specific time. When you first open the Calendar, it opens in Day view, showing today's date. You can switch to a different date by clicking that date on the **Date Navigator**, a small calendar in the upper right of the Calendar window. You view your appointments for a particular day by looking at the **Appointment area**, the section of the Calendar that resembles a yellow pad of paper divided into time slots. You also use the Appointment area to enter new appointments. To enter a new appointment, double-click a time slot to open the **Appointment form**, where you provide information about the appointment. If your appointment recurs regularly, you can use the Recurrence button of the Appointment form to set a specific recurring time. When you do this, **recurring appointments** are automatically added to the Calendar.

To move a non-recurring appointment to a different time, drag it to a new time slot in the Appointment area. To move a non-recurring appointment to the same time on a different day, drag it to a new date on the Date Navigator.

Activity Steps

1. Start Outlook, then if necessary, choose your **Profile name**, click **OK**, enter your **password**, then click **OK**

2. Click the **Calendar icon** 📅 on the Outlook Bar
   See Figure 2-1.

3. Use the Date Navigator to navigate to June 2003, then click **June 16** on the Date Navigator

4. Double-click the **8:00 am time slot** to open the Appointment form, type **Staff meeting** in the Subject box, press **[Tab]**, type **Siberian Conference Room**, click the **second End time list arrow** (in the time section), then click **9:00 AM (1 hour)**
   See Figure 2-2.

5. Click **Recurrence** on the toolbar to open the Appointment Recurrence dialog box, select the **Monthly option button** in the Recurrence pattern section, select **the third Monday of every 1 month(s) option button**, then click **OK**

6. Click **Save and Close** on the toolbar
   The bell icon indicates that an alarm is set for this appointment, and the circular arrows icon shows that the appointment recurs.

7. Click **Today** on the toolbar

Figure 2-1: Calendar showing today's date in Day view

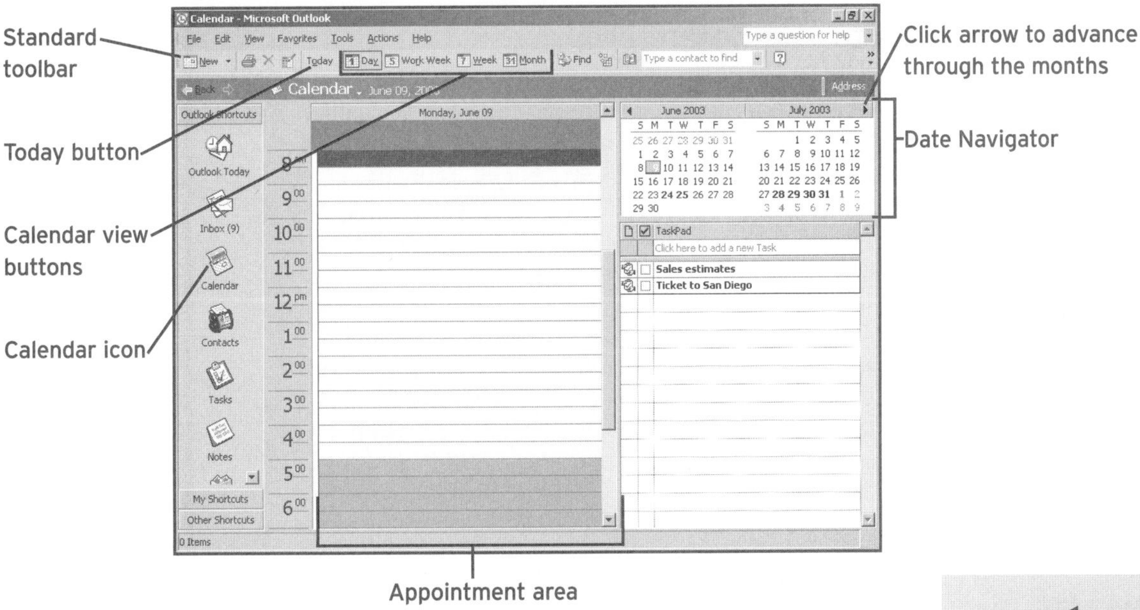

Standard toolbar

Today button

Calendar view buttons

Calendar icon

Click arrow to advance through the months

Date Navigator

Appointment area

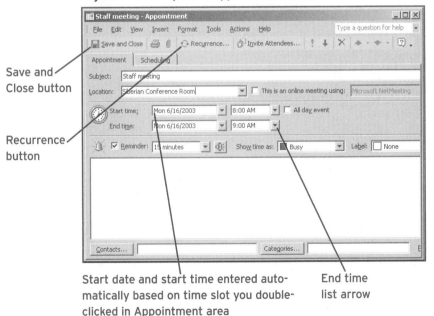

Figure 2-2: Completed Appointment form

Save and Close button

Recurrence button

Start date and start time entered automatically based on time slot you double-clicked in Appointment area

End time list arrow

Skill Set 2

Scheduling

Add Appointments, Meetings, and Events to the Calendar

Add Events to the Calendar

Sometimes you need to schedule full-day activities, called **events**, in Outlook. Entering a new event in the Calendar is much like entering a new appointment. You use the Appointment form to specify the subject and location of the appointment, as well as other information. To save yourself the trouble of setting start and end times, you can use the All day event check box to specify that the event will take up an entire day. You can also set a reminder alarm or specify that the Calendar visually highlight the event in a particular way so that colleagues who view your Calendar can see whether you are free, busy, out of the office, or have a tentative appointment. You can even color-code events so that you can see at a glance which events are personal, business-related, or require preparation. You can also use the Appointment form to specify that an appointment is private, which will make it visible only to you, not to others who have access to your Calendar.

To enter appointments in the Calendar without opening the Appointment form, click a time slot in the Appointment area, then type the subject for the appointment.

Activity Steps

1. Click the **Calendar icon** on the Outlook Bar, if necessary, then click the **New Appointment button** on the toolbar
   The Appointment form opens with the Appointment tab displayed.

2. Maximize the Appointment form, if necessary, type **Vacation day** in the Subject box, press **[Tab]**, then type **Peace and Tranquility Day Spa** in the Location box

3. Click the **Start time list arrow**, then click **next Wednesday's date** on the Start time Calendar

4. Click the **All day event check box**

5. Verify that there is a check mark in the Reminder check box, click the **Reminder list arrow**, click **1 day**, click the **Show time as list arrow**, click **Out of Office**, click the **Label list arrow**, then click **Personal**

6. Type the following in the text box below the Reminder check box: **Package includes massage, yoga class, spa lunch, and sea salt body scrub.**, then click the **Private check box** in the lower-right corner of the form
   See Figure 2-3.

7. Click **Save and Close** on the toolbar, then click **next Wednesday's date** on the Date Navigator
   A green shaded box shows the All day event. *See Figure 2-4.*

8. Click **Today** on the toolbar

Figure 2-3: Completed Appointment form for All day event

Save and Close button

Choose this label to apply green shading to appointment

Reminder list arrow

Click to mark appointment as private

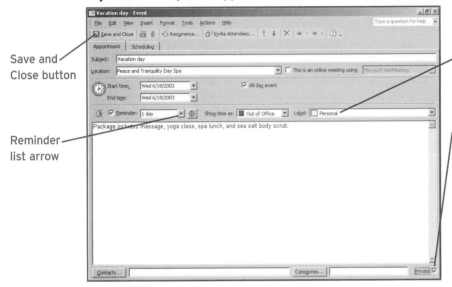

Figure 2-4: Calendar showing All day event

Today button

New All day event

Bell icon indicates alarm will sound as a reminder

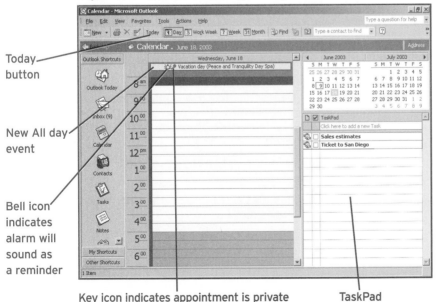

Key icon indicates appointment is private

TaskPad

extra!

Viewing tasks in the TaskPad

Below the Date Navigator in the Calendar window is the TaskPad, which shows a list of the tasks stored in your Tasks folder. The tasks shown in Figure 2-4 are the task item Project Files that you copied in the Getting Started skill set. If you have additional tasks in your Tasks folder, then they will appear in the list, too. To change the way tasks appear in the TaskPad, click View on the menu bar, point to TaskPad view, then click a selection from the submenu.

Skill Set 2

Scheduling

Add Appointments, Meetings, and Events to the Calendar

Schedule Meetings and Invite Attendees

Trying to schedule a meeting with a large group of busy people can be both frustrating and time-consuming. It often seems impossible to find a meeting time that works for everyone. Outlook has tools that can help save you time and make scheduling meetings much easier. To invite attendees to a meeting you use the **Meeting Request form** available in the Calendar. You use the **Appointment tab** of this form to enter details such as the subject and location for the meeting and to select attendees you want to invite to the meeting. You can also add additional notes for the attendees and set a label color for the meeting so that attendees know what type of meeting it is. You use the **Scheduling tab** to view the schedules of all the attendees, and then set a meeting time that works for all. You can manually set a meeting time or specify that Outlook automatically schedule a meeting at the next available time that works for everyone. Once you've filled in all the necessary information in the Meeting Request form, you send it to the attendees.

Click the Importance: High button on the toolbar to let attendees know that a particular meeting is a crucial one. Click the Importance: Low button on the toolbar to communicate that a meeting is not that important.

Activity Steps

1. Click the **Calendar icon** 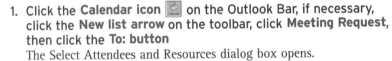 on the Outlook Bar, if necessary, click the **New list arrow** on the toolbar, click **Meeting Request**, then click the **To: button**
   The Select Attendees and Resources dialog box opens.

2. Click **Bettijean Riley** in the Name list, click **Required**, click **Ridley Carson** in the Name list, click **Optional**, then click **OK**

3. Type **Product launch planning meeting** in the Subject box, press **Tab**, type **Bengal Conference Room** in the Location box, then click the **Scheduling tab** (If a dialog box opens asking if you want to join the Microsoft Office Internet Free/Busy Service, click **Cancel**)

4. Use the horizontal scroll bar on the time grid to navigate to **tomorrow's date**

5. Click the **11:00 time slot** anywhere on the grid, then drag the **red border** of the time slot box to **12:00**
   See Figure 2-5.

6. Click the **Appointment tab**, then type **Bettijean, please prepare a competitive analysis for this meeting.** in the large text box in the bottom half of the screen

7. Click the **Label list arrow**, click **Needs Preparation**, compare your screen with Figure 2-6, then click **Send** on the toolbar

Figure 2-5: Scheduling tab of Meeting Request form

Your name
should appear
here

Icon indicates
attendee is
required

Icon indicates
attendee is
optional

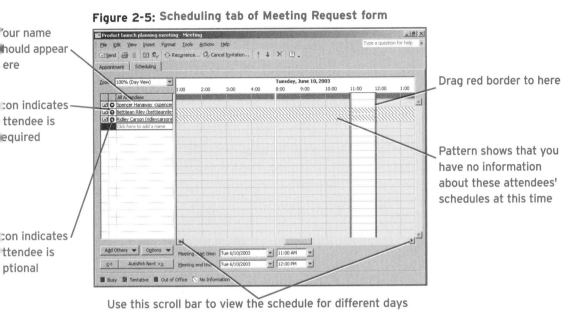

Drag red border to here

Pattern shows that you
have no information
about these attendees'
schedules at this time

Use this scroll bar to view the schedule for different days

Figure 2-6: Completed Appointment tab of Meeting Request form

Click to send
the meeting
request to
people listed
in the To: box

Importance:
High button

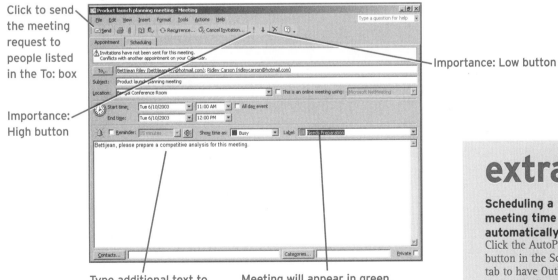

Importance: Low button

Type additional text to
attendees here

Meeting will appear in green,
indicating preparation is needed

extra!

**Scheduling a
meeting time
automatically**
Click the AutoPick Next
button in the Scheduling
tab to have Outlook
automatically set the
meeting for the next
available time slot that
works for all invitees.

Skill Set 2
Scheduling

Add Appointments, Meetings, and Events to the Calendar
Schedule Resources for Meetings

Sometimes a meeting requires special equipment, such as a flip chart, a projector, or a monitor. You can use Outlook to reserve this kind of item, called a **resource**, for a meeting. To do this, you invite the resource you need to the meeting, just as you would invite a person. However, this feature is not available to everyone using Outlook. In order to schedule resources for a meeting, you must have Outlook running on a Microsoft Exchange Server. In addition, each resource you want to invite must have its own e-mail box on the server. If both these requirements are met, then you can schedule resources. To schedule a resource, you use the Plan a Meeting form to set a time for your meeting, and then use the Select Attendees and Resources dialog box to choose the resources you want. You then use the Meeting Request form to invite all the attendees and resources to the meeting.

Sometimes, certain resources are restricted so that only a select group of people have the right to use them. If you try to schedule a resource you do not have permission to use, the resource will automatically reject your meeting request.

Activity Steps

1. Click the **Calendar icon** on the Outlook Bar, if necessary, click **Actions** on the menu bar, then click **Plan a Meeting**

2. Click **Add Others**, then click **Add from Address Book**
   If your school or company is connected to a Global Address List, you will see a list of resources in the Name list. *See Figure 2-7.*

3. Click **Bettijean Riley** in the Name list, then click **Required**

4. If you see a list of Resources in the Name list, click **one of the Resources in the list**, then click **Resources** (If you don't see a list of resources, click one of the names, then click **Resources**)
   The e-mail address of the person responsible for the resource you clicked appears in the Resources box.

5. Click **OK** (If a dialog box opens asking if you want to join the Microsoft Office Internet Free/Busy Service, click **Cancel**)

6. Use the horizontal scroll bar so that 3:00 tomorrow appears on the time grid, click **3:00**, then click **Make Meeting** at the bottom of the Plan a Meeting form

7. Type **Brainstorming meeting** in the Subject box, type **Siberian Conference Room** in the Location box, then click **Send**
   The Meeting form closes. The Plan a Meeting form shows the day of your newly planned meeting with the 3:00 time slot shaded in blue. *See Figure 2-8.*

8. Click **Close**, click **tomorrow's date** on the Date Navigator to view the new meeting, then click the **Today button** on the toolbar

Figure 2-7: Select Attendees and Resources dialog box

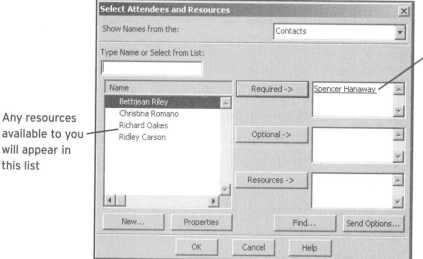

Your name should appear here

Any resources available to you will appear in this list

Figure 2-8: Plan a Meeting form with new meeting

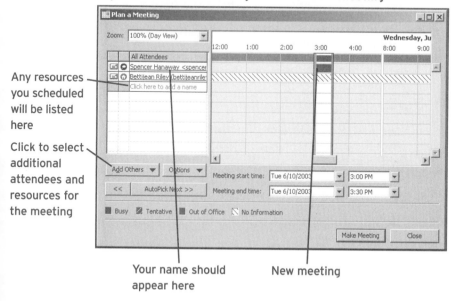

Any resources you scheduled will be listed here

Click to select additional attendees and resources for the meeting

Your name should appear here

New meeting

extra!

Using the Microsoft Office Free/Busy Service

If you have Internet access and would like to let others know when you have free blocks of time, you can publish your available and busy times to the Microsoft Office Internet Free/Busy Service, a Web-based service offered through Microsoft. Doing this service lets other users plan meetings and schedule a time that works for you. For more Information, visit *http://freebusy. office.microsoft.com/ freebusy/freebusy.dll on the Web.*

Skill Set 2

Scheduling

Apply Conditional Formats to the Outlook Calendar

Apply Conditional Formats to the Calendar

If your Calendar is packed with appointments, it can be overwhelming to look at your schedule for a particular day and see everything you have to do. You can ease your mind and help make sense of your day by applying color-coding labels to each appointment. Color coding lets you see at a glance what kind of appointments are ahead for the day or week. For instance, you could label an appointment as Personal, Important, or Travel Required. You can assign a label to an appointment when you first create it, using the Appointment form. However, if your Calendar already contains lots of different appointments that are not color-labeled, you can apply labels to them using the Automatic Formatting dialog box. In this dialog box, you create rules for labeling a particular type of appointment. For instance, you could create a new rule called Dance Class and specify that the Personal label be applied to all appointments that have the words "dance class" in the Subject box.

Step 4
You can also open the Automatic Formatting dialog box by clicking View on the menu bar, pointing to Current View, clicking Customize Current View, then clicking Automatic Formatting in the View Summary dialog box.

Activity Steps

1. Click the **Calendar icon** on the Outlook Bar, if necessary, then click **next Thursday's date** on the Date Navigator

2. Click the **New Appointment button**, type **Board of Directors Meeting** in the Subject box, press **Tab**, type **Bengal Conference Room**, set the Start time at **10:00 AM**, set the End time at **12:00 PM**, then click **Save and Close**

3. Click the **Calendar Coloring button** on the toolbar, then click **Automatic Formatting**

4. Click **Add**, type **Board of Directors** in the Name box, click the **Label list arrow**, then click **Important**
   See Figure 2-9.

5. Click **Condition**, type **Board of Directors** in the Search for the words text box, then click **OK** two times
   The Board of Directors appointment that you created now appears in red with the conditional formatting applied, indicating it is an important meeting.
   See Figure 2-10.

6. Click the **Today button** on the toolbar

Figure 2-9: Automatic Formatting dialog box with new rule added

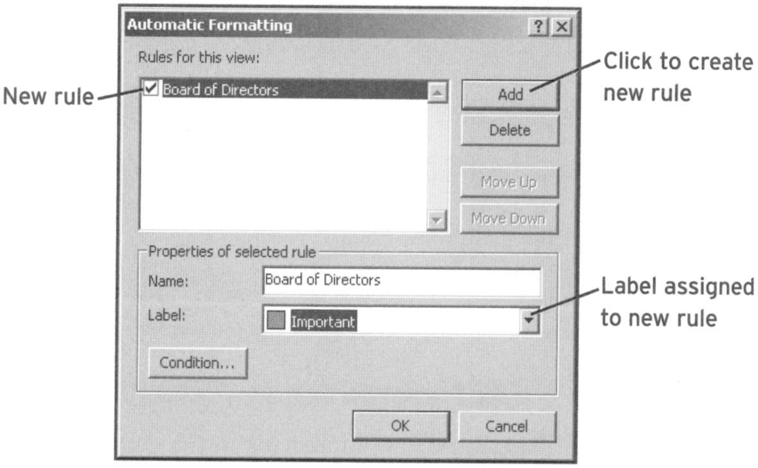

New rule ─

Click to create
new rule

Label assigned
to new rule

Figure 2-10: Calendar showing appointment with conditional formatting applied

Color-coded
appointment
with conditional
formatting
applied

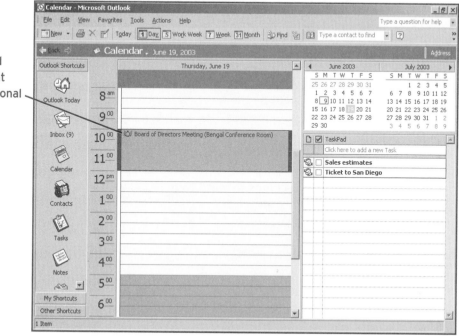

Skill Set 2
Scheduling

Respond to Meeting Requests
Accept Meeting Requests

If you are involved in many projects, you will likely be asked to many meetings. If someone using Outlook needs you at a meeting, they will send a **meeting request** to your Inbox. A meeting request tells you the subject and location of the meeting as well as the date and time. You can quickly check your availability for a particular meeting by using the Calendar button on the Meeting Request form toolbar. This button opens your Calendar to the date of the meeting with the meeting inserted in the proposed time slot. You accept a meeting using the Accept button on the toolbar. When you accept, the meeting is automatically added to your Calendar. You can also include an additional message with your acceptance.

If you are not sure you can attend a particular meeting, you can accept it on a tentative basis by clicking the Tentative button on the Meeting form toolbar. Doing this tells the meeting organizer that you might not be able to attend. It also automatically enters the meeting in your Calendar.

Activity Steps

1. Click the **Inbox icon** on the Outlook Bar, then double-click the **Annual Review Meeting message** from Ridley Carson
   The Meeting form opens.

2. Maximize the Meeting form, if necessary, read the message, then click the **Calendar button** [Calendar...] on the toolbar
   The Calendar opens on top of the Meeting form, showing the date of the proposed meeting.
   See Figure 2-11.

3. Click the **Close button** in the Calendar window, then click **Accept** on the Meeting form toolbar

4. Click the **Edit the response before sending option button**, then click **OK**
   The Meeting Response form opens, with the insertion point in the response text box.

5. Type **I look forward to meeting with you.**
   See Figure 2-12.

6. Click **Send**

Figure 2-11: Calendar window open on top of Meeting form

Click to accept meeting

Click to accept meeting on a tentative basis

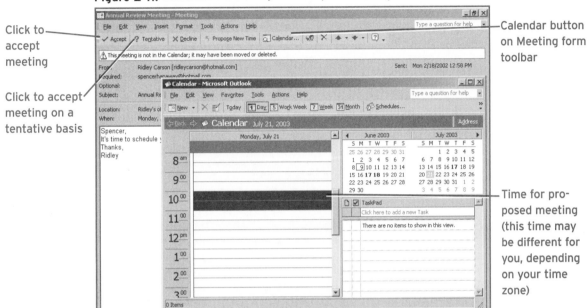

Calendar button on Meeting form toolbar

Time for proposed meeting (this time may be different for you, depending on your time zone)

Figure 2-12: Accepted Meeting Response form with edited reply

Click to accept meeting and send reply message

Type additional text here

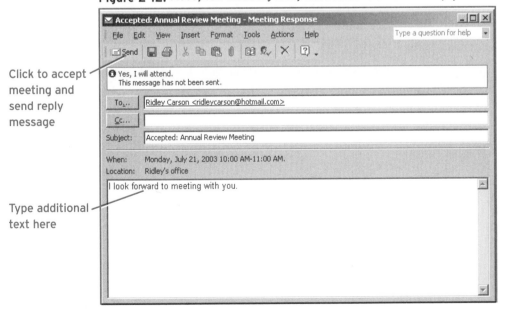

Skill Set 2
Scheduling

Respond to Meeting Requests
Decline Meeting Requests

If you receive a large number of meeting requests, or if you have a full schedule, you will probably not be able to attend all meetings to which you are invited. You can decline a meeting request using the Decline button in the Meeting form. You also have the option of including an additional message. When you decline, Outlook does not add the meeting to your Calendar.

Activity Steps

Step 1
If you have many messages in your Inbox and can't find this particular message, click the From column heading to sort by the name of the Sender, then scroll to find the messages from Ridley Carson.

1. Click the **Inbox icon** on the Outlook Bar, if necessary, then double-click the **Annual Corporate Run Informational Meeting message** in the Inbox
   The message information appears in the Meeting form.
   See Figure 2-13.

2. Read the information about this meeting in the Meeting form, then click the **Calendar button** on the Meeting form toolbar
   Your Calendar shows that you have no meetings that conflict with the proposed meeting time. You also need to check to see if you have a conflict on August 15, the day of the race.

3. Use the Date Navigator to navigate to August 2003, click **August 15, 2003** on the Date Navigator, then scroll to view 12 am in the Appointment area
   The Calendar shows that you are taking a vacation day on August 15.
   See Figure 2-14.

4. Click the Calendar window **Close button**, then click the **Decline button** on the toolbar
   An alert box opens containing three option buttons.

5. Click the **Edit the response before sending option button**, then click **OK**

6. Type **Sorry, I will be on vacation on August 15 so I cannot run in this race. Good luck!**

7. Click **Send**

Figure 2-13: Meeting Request form

Decline button

Subject of proposed meeting

Message from sender

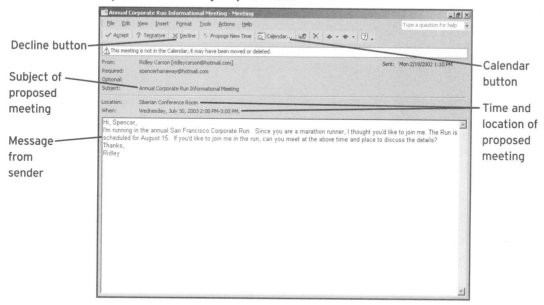

Calendar button

Time and location of proposed meeting

Figure 2-14: Calendar showing all-day event

All day event conflicts with proposed subject of meeting

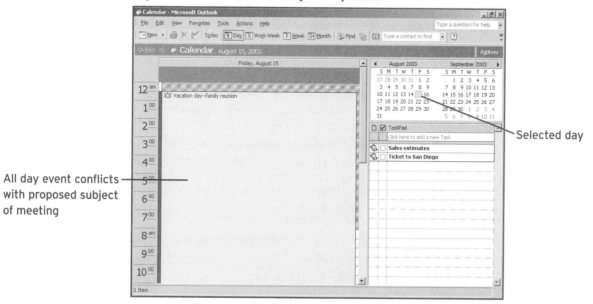

Selected day

Skill Set 2

Scheduling

Respond to Meeting Requests

Propose New Meeting Times

You might get invited to an important meeting that you need to attend, but the proposed time conflicts with another previously scheduled appointment. When you receive such a meeting request in Outlook, you have the option of proposing new times for the meeting. To propose new times for a meeting, you use the Propose New Time button on the Meeting form toolbar. You can then view the schedules of the other attendees (if available to you), specify a different start and end time, and then use the Propose Time button to communicate your proposed new times to the sender. When you do this, the meeting is entered into your Calendar at the originally proposed time and is marked as tentative.

Step 4
You can also adjust the time in the Propose New Time form by dragging the red and green lines in the grid area.

Activity Steps

1. Click the **Inbox icon** 📁 on the Outlook Bar, if necessary, then double-click the **Maternity Tea Marketing Strategy Meeting message** from Ridley Carson

2. Click **Calendar** on the Meeting form toolbar
   If your computer clock is set to Eastern Standard Time, the Calendar shows that you have a dentist appointment that conflicts with the meeting.

3. Click the **Calendar Close button**, then click **Propose New Time** (If a dialog box opens asking if you want to join the Microsoft Office Internet Free/Busy Service, click **Cancel**)

4. Click the **second Meeting start time list arrow**, then click **11:00 AM**
   See Figure 2-15.

5. Click **Propose Time**
   The New Time Proposed form opens with text in the Subject box automatically included.

6. Type your e-mail address in the Cc: box, then click **Send** (If you are using an ISP, click **Send/Receive** two times to transfer your messages from your Outbox to the ISP's server and then to your Inbox)
   The message you just wrote should appear in your Inbox, with the new proposed time in the text area.

7. Double-click the **New Time Proposed message** in your Inbox
   See Figure 2-16.

8. Close the message form

Figure 2-15: Propose New Time form with new proposed start and end times

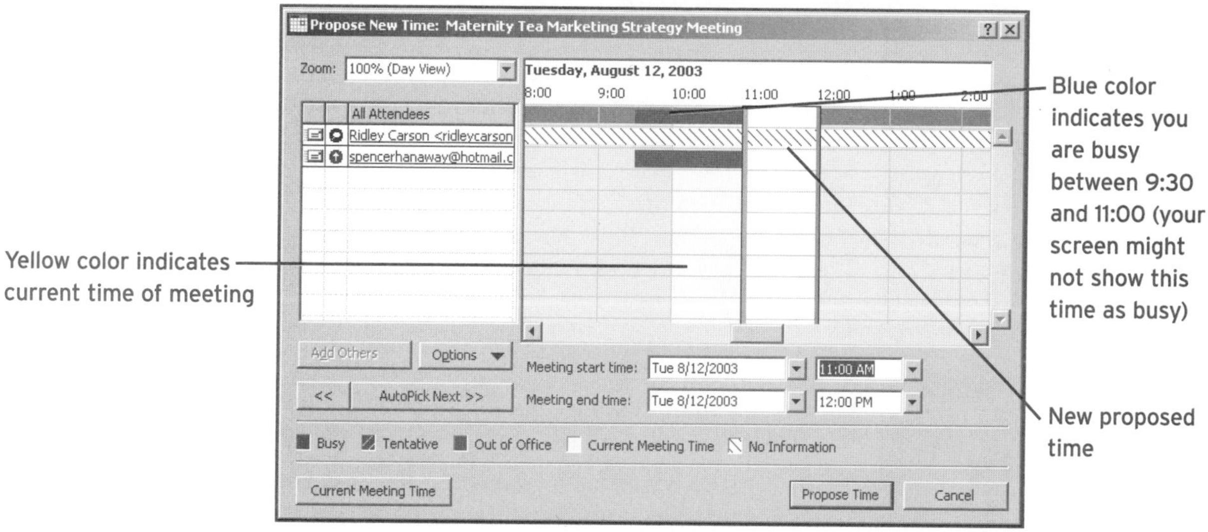

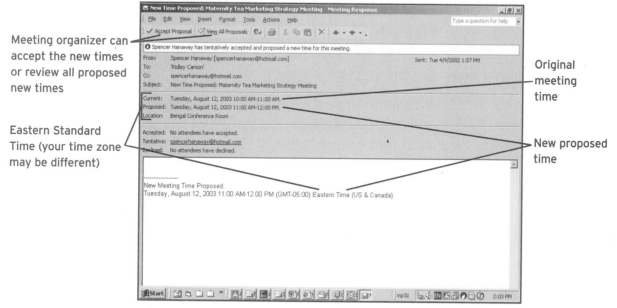

Yellow color indicates current time of meeting

Blue color indicates you are busy between 9:30 and 11:00 (your screen might not show this time as busy)

New proposed time

Figure 2-16: New Time Proposed Meeting Response form

Meeting organizer can accept the new times or review all proposed new times

Eastern Standard Time (your time zone may be different)

Original meeting time

New proposed time

Skill Set 2

Scheduling

Use Categories to Manage Appointments
Assign Categories to Appointments

When your Calendar is jammed with appointments, it's helpful to group them into different categories so that you can look at related appointments together. Outlook comes with a variety of predefined categories that you can assign to any appointment, including Personal, Business, Ideas, and many others. You can also create your own categories. For instance, if you are organizing a food drive, you could create the category Food Drive and assign this name to all the appointments related to it. You can also assign multiple categories to a single appointment. You assign, view, and add categories using the Categories dialog box, which you open from the Appointment form.

Activity Steps

To view your appointments by category, click View on the menu bar, point to Current View, then click By Category.

1. Click the **Calendar icon** 📅 on the Outlook Bar, click **tomorrow's date** on the Date Navigator, then click **New**

2. Type **Competitive analysis for Bali Tea product line** in the Subject box, press **Tab**, then type **My office** in the Location box

3. Set the Start time at **2:00 PM** and the End time at **3:00 PM**

4. Click **Categories** to open the Categories dialog box

5. Type **Bali Tea Product Development** in the Item(s) belong to these categories text box, then click **Add to List**
The new category is added to the list and is automatically selected. *See Figure 2-17.*

6. Click the **Competition** check box, then click **OK**
The two categories you selected appear in the Categories box. *See Figure 2-18.*

7. Click **Save and Close** on the Appointment form toolbar

Figure 2-17: Categories dialog box with new category added

Type new category here

New category added to list and selected

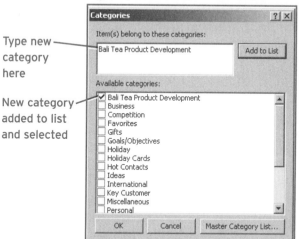

Figure 2-18: Appointment form showing selected categories in Categories box

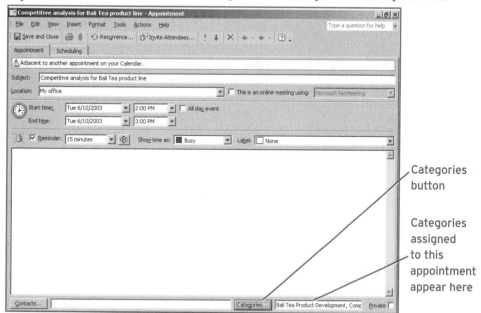

Categories button

Categories assigned to this appointment appear here

Skill Set 2
Scheduling

Print Calendars
Print the Calendar in Different Views

Because carrying your computer around with you is not always practical, you will probably find it helpful to print your Calendar on occasion, so that you can keep track of your appointments while on the go. Just as you can view your Calendar in different ways, you can also print it in a variety of formats. The format you choose is called a **print style**, and these include Daily, Weekly, and Monthly, among others. You use the Print dialog box to select a print style and a date range. For each print style, you can choose from a variety of formatting options using the Page Setup dialog box, accessible from the Print dialog box. For instance, you can choose to print a lined area for writing notes, or you can change the font for headings. To save paper, it's a good idea to preview your Calendar with your chosen settings before printing.

To print an entire month of the Calendar, click Monthly Style in the Print style area of the Print dialog box, then click OK.

Activity Steps

1. Click the **Calendar icon** on the Outlook Bar, if necessary, then use the Date Navigator to navigate to **July 28, 2003**

2. Click **File** on the menu bar, then click **Print**
   The Print dialog box opens, with the Daily Style selected in the Print style list.
   See Figure 2-19.

3. Click the **Preview button**, view the daily schedule, click **Page Setup** on the toolbar, click the **Notes area (lined) check box** in the Options section, click the **Paper tab**, click the **Landscape option button**, then click **Print Preview**

4. Click **Print** on the Preview toolbar, then click **OK** in the Print dialog box

5. Click **File** on the menu bar, click **Print** to open the Print dialog box, click **Weekly Style** in the Print style list box, click **Preview**, then click in the upper-left (Monday) square
   The top half of the Calendar is magnified, making it possible to read the appointments for Monday and Thursday.
   See Figure 2-20.

6. Click **Print** on the Preview toolbar, then click **OK** in the Print dialog box

Figure 2-19: Print dialog box

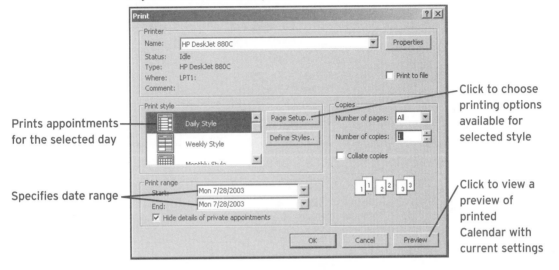

Prints appointments for the selected day

Click to choose printing options available for selected style

Specifies date range

Click to view a preview of printed Calendar with current settings

Figure 2-20: Print Preview window showing top half of weekly calendar

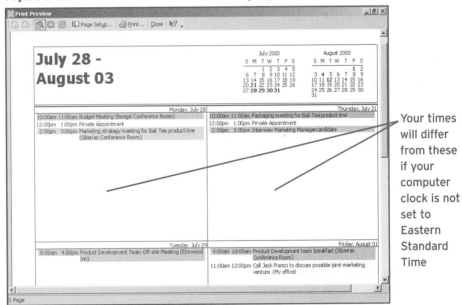

Your times will differ from these if your computer clock is not set to Eastern Standard Time

Skill Set 2

Scheduling

Target Your Skills

1 Use Figure 2-21 as a guide. Send a meeting request to Ridley Carson, Bettijean Riley, and yourself for the date, time, and location shown. Mark the meeting as private. Send the meeting request. Open the meeting request in your Inbox.

2 Using Figure 2-22 as a guide, enter the following appointments in your Calendar on the date shown:
9:00 Inventory Meeting
12:00 Lunch with Joe (mark as private)
3:00 Write inventory report
5:00 Farewell party
Specify a location and apply appropriate labels for each. Create a category called Inventory that has the Important label. Then, use conditional formatting to apply the Important label to all appointments that have "inventory" in the subject line. Print the Calendar using the settings shown.

Figure 2-21

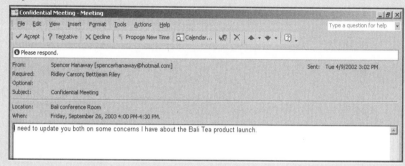

Figure 2-22

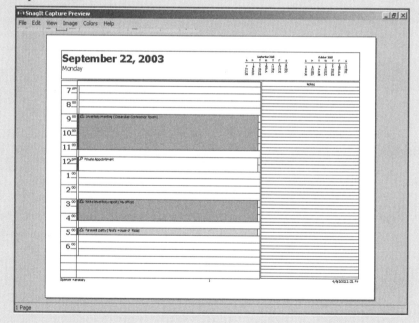

Skill List

1. Move messages between folders
2. Search for messages
3. Save messages in alternate file formats
4. Use categories to manage messages
5. Set message options

If you rely on e-mail for many of your daily communications, you might find yourself getting overwhelmed by a huge volume of messages. To avoid having an overcrowded Inbox, it's important that you organize the messages you want to save so that they are easy to retrieve. Outlook provides many tools for managing your messages. In this skill set, you'll learn to create folders to help you organize your messages into logical groups. You'll also learn to move messages between folders and to find messages by specifying search text or assigning categories. You'll learn how to save message files in different formats so they can be viewed on computers where Outlook is not installed, and how to archive old messages to free up space in your Inbox and other folders. Finally, you'll learn to modify the settings for delivering messages.

Skill Set 3
Managing Messages

Move Messages Between Folders
Move a Message to a Different Folder

If you receive a large amount of e-mail on a regular basis, your Inbox can fill up quickly. You will probably delete many old messages, but you may also want to keep some. To help you quickly locate the messages you need, you can create folders in which to store related messages. For instance, if you are coordinating all the arrangements for an upcoming sales meeting, you could create a folder called Sales Meeting and place all the messages related to the sales meeting in this folder. You use the Move Items dialog box to move messages to an existing folder or to create a new folder. If you create a new folder, that folder will be contained by the selected folder in the Move Items dialog box.

Activity

1. Start Outlook, then if necessary, choose your **Profile name**, click **OK**, enter your **password**, click **OK**, click the **Inbox icon** on the Outlook Bar, then click the **Subject column heading** to sort your messages by the Subject field

2. Click the **RE: Regional meeting message from Linda Miller**, press and hold **[Shift]**, then click the original **Regional meeting message** from Stephen James so that a total of four messages with Regional meeting in the Subject line are selected (You might have to scroll to see all four messages)

To move a message using the mouse, drag the message from the Inbox to the desired folder in the Folder List.

3. Click the **Move to Folder button** on the Standard toolbar, then click **Move to Folder**
   The Move Items dialog box opens.
   See Figure 3-1.

4. Click **Inbox**, if necessary, click **New** to open the Create New Folder dialog box, type **Regional Meeting**, then click **OK**

5. Click **No** in the dialog box that opens asking if you would like to add a shortcut to this folder to your Outlook Bar, then click **OK**

6. Click the **plus sign** next to the Inbox icon in the Folder List, if necessary, then click the **Regional Meeting folder** in the Folder list
   See Figure 3-2.

7. Click the **Inbox icon** on the Outlook Bar, click the **Folder List Close button**, then click the **Received column heading** to sort your messages by date

Figure 3-1: Move Items dialog box

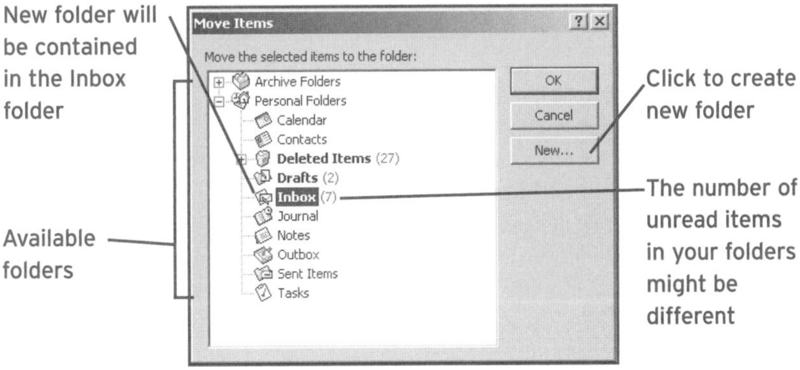

New folder will be contained in the Inbox folder

Available folders

Click to create new folder

The number of unread items in your folders might be different

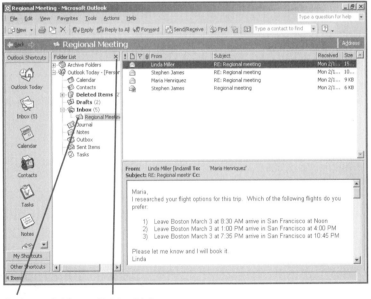

Figure 3-2: Messages moved to new folder

Selected new folder

Folder List Close button

extra!

Using the Move to Folder menu to move an item

Clicking the Move to Folder button opens a menu showing a list of available Outlook folders. Click a folder name on the menu to move a selected item to that folder. Any new folder you create or use is added as a folder name to the top of this menu.

Skill Set 3

Managing Messages

Search for Messages

Search for a Message

If you have a large number of messages in your Inbox or another folder and want to find one message in particular, it's not very practical to look for the message by scanning the contents of a folder. The **Find bar** makes it fast and easy to locate messages. You can use the Find bar to specify the text you want to locate and the folder where you want to look. The search text you specify is not case-sensitive and can be located in the message body or in the subject field. This means that you can find a particular message even if the only characteristic you remember about it was a specific word used in the message body. To open the Find bar, you use the Find button on the Standard toolbar.

Step 2
You can also open the Find bar by pressing [Ctrl][E], or by clicking Tools on the menu bar, then clicking Find.

Activity

1. Click the **Inbox icon** on the Outlook Bar, if necessary

2. Click the **Find button** on the Standard toolbar
   The Find bar appears above your list of messages.

3. Type **Denver** in the Look for box, then click **Find Now**
   All of the messages in the Inbox that have Denver in the Subject line or message body appear.
   See Figure 3-3.

4. Click the **Clear button** on the Find bar
   You could do another search, or close the Find bar.

5. Click the **Find button**
   The Find bar closes.

Figure 3-3: Messages in Inbox that contain the word "Denver"

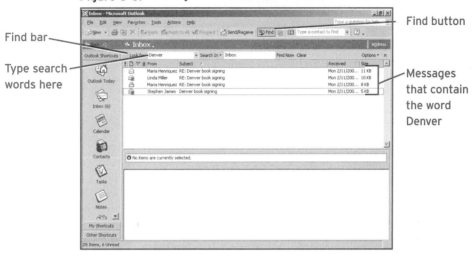

Find button

Find bar

Type search
words here

Messages
that contain
the word
Denver

extra!

Using the Advanced Find feature

You can use the Advanced Find dialog box, shown in Figure 3-4, to refine your search for a particular message or other Outlook item. For instance, you can search for messages from a particular sender or to a recipient. You can also specify that the search results contain only items sent, received, created, or modified in a particular time frame. If you assign categories to your messages or items, you can also set the search criteria for a specified category. You can also specify that the search results contain only read or unread messages, attachments or no attachments, or have a specific Importance level assigned to them. To open the Advanced Find dialog box, click Options on the Find bar, then click Advanced Find.

Figure 3-4: Advanced Find dialog box

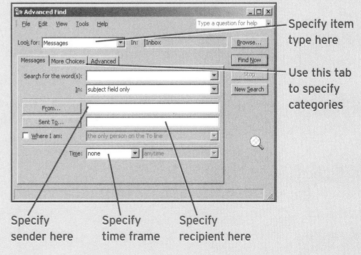

Specify item
type here

Use this tab
to specify
categories

Specify
sender here

Specify
time frame

Specify
recipient here

Skill Set 3
Managing Messages

Save Messages in Alternate File Formats
Save Messages as HTML files

By default, messages and all other items created in Outlook are saved with a .msg file extension. There might be times when you want to save an e-mail message in a different file format. For instance, if you need to view your message files on a computer that is not running Outlook, and want to preserve the formatting of the message, you can save it as an .htm file. When you save a file as an htm file, all the formatting is preserved. To save a file in .htm format, you use the Save As dialog box. When you open a message file in .htm format, it opens in your default browser.

Activity Steps

1. Click the **Inbox icon** on the Outlook Bar, if necessary, click the **Flight to Atlanta message** from Linda Miller, click **File** on the menu bar, then click **Save As**
   See Figure 3-5.

2. Verify that **HTML (*.htm; *.html)** is selected in the Save as type list box, then navigate to the folder where your Project Files are stored

3. Click **Save**

4. Click **Other Shortcuts** on the Outlook Bar, click **My Computer**, then navigate to the folder where your Project Files are stored

5. Double-click the **Flight to Atlanta.htm file** you just saved
   The message opens in Internet Explorer.
   See Figure 3-6.

6. Click the **Internet Explorer Close button**, then click the **Outlook program button** on the taskbar

7. Click the **Outlook Shortcuts** on the Outlook Bar

Figure 3-5: Save As dialog box

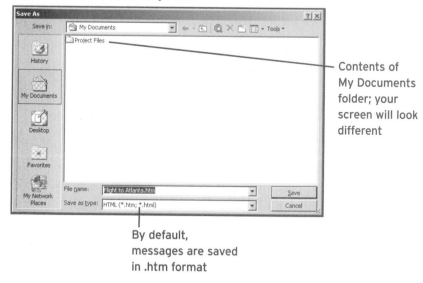

Contents of
My Documents
folder; your
screen will look
different

By default,
messages are saved
in .htm format

Figure 3-6: Saved message in .htm format in Internet Explorer

Location of file
appears here

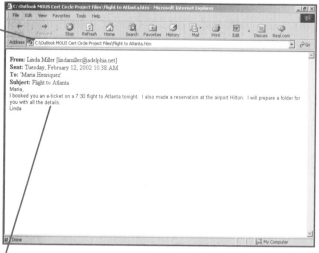

Formatting of
original message
is preserved

extra!

Deleting messages
To delete messages that
you no longer want,
select the unwanted
messages in the Inbox
or any other folder, then
press [Del] or click the
Delete button on the
toolbar. Messages that
you delete are not
permanently removed
from your computer,
however; they are
moved to the Deleted
Items folder. To clear
the Deleted Items
folder, right-click the
Deleted Items folder in
the Folder List, click
Empty "Deleted Items"
Folder on the shortcut
menu, then click Yes.

Skill Set 3

Managing Messages

Save Messages in Alternate File Formats

Save Messages as Text Files

There might be times when you would like to save a message file in **Text Only format**, which saves the text of a message but does not preserve the formatting of the original message. Saving a message as a text file in Text Only format is often a good idea if you need to view a message on another computer that does not have Outlook installed, and if you are not concerned about preserving the original formatting. To save a message file as a text file, you use the Save As dialog box. Files saved as text files have a .txt extension. When you open a message file that has been saved as a text file, it opens in Notepad by default.

By default, all messages you create in Outlook are in HTML format. To change the default message format, click Tools on the menu bar, click Options, click the Mail Format tab, click the Compose in this message format list arrow, then click the format you want.

Activity

1. Click the **Inbox icon** on the Outlook Bar, if necessary

2. Click the **Flight to Atlanta message from Linda Miller**, click **File** on the menu bar, then click **Save As**

3. Click the **Save as type list arrow**, click **Text Only (*.txt)**, then navigate to the folder where your Project Files are stored
   See Figure 3-7.

4. Click **Save**

5. Click **Other Shortcuts** on the Outlook Bar, click **My Computer**, then navigate to the folder where your Project Files are stored

6. Double-click the **Flight to Atlanta.txt file** you just saved
   The message opens in Notepad. Only part of the message text fits in the NotePad window because Word Wrap is turned off.

7. Click **Format** on the menu bar, then click **Word Wrap**
   All the message text now fits in the Notepad window.
   See Figure 3-8.

8. Click the **Notepad Close button**, click the **Outlook program button** on the taskbar, then click **Outlook Shortcuts** on the Outlook Bar

Figure 3-7: Save As dialog box

Save as type
list arrow

Figure 3-8: Message saved as text file opened in Notepad

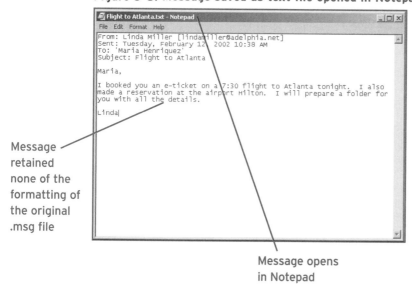

Message retained none of the formatting of the original .msg file

Message opens in Notepad

extra!

Understanding where items are stored

Unless you use the Microsoft Exchange Server, any Outlook items you create or receive or any folders you create in Outlook are saved to a data file known as a **Personal Folders** file on your computer's hard drive. The default data file to which items are stored is Outlook.pst. If you use a Microsoft Exchange Server, your Outlook items are stored on the server.

Skill Set 3

Managing Messages

Use Categories to Manage Messages

Assign Categories to Messages

To make finding messages or other items easier, you can assign categories to them. A **category** is a keyword or phrase that helps you organize items so you can sort them in meaningful ways. Outlook comes with a variety of predefined categories that you can assign to messages and other items, including Business, Personal, Miscellaneous, and many others. You can assign predefined categories to your messages, or you can create new categories appropriate for your specific needs. For example, you might want to create a category called Company Meeting and assign all the messages relating to the company meeting to it. You could then search for all the messages that have the Company Meeting category assigned to them. You use the Advanced Find dialog box to search for messages assigned to a particular category.

Step 5
You can also open the Advanced Find dialog box by clicking Find on the Standard toolbar to open the Find bar, clicking Options on the Find bar, then clicking Advanced Find.

Activity

1. Click the **Inbox icon** on the Outlook Bar, if necessary, then click the **Subject column heading** in the Inbox to sort the messages by subject

2. Scroll to locate the four messages that contain the words **Denver book signing**, then select all four of these messages

3. Click **Edit** on the menu bar, then click **Categories**
   A list of available categories appears. You can add a new one. *See Figure 3-9.*

4. Click the **Item(s) belong to these categories text box**, type **Book Signings**, then click **Add to List**
   The Book Signings category now appears in the list and is checked. You can use this new category to search for related messages.

5. Click **OK**, click **Tools** on the menu bar, then click **Advanced Find**

6. Click the **More Choices tab**, click **Categories**, click **Book Signings** in the Available Categories list, click **OK**, then click **Find Now**
   The four messages to which you applied the Book Signings category appear at the bottom of the dialog box.
   See Figure 3-10.

7. Click the **Advanced Find dialog box Close button**, then click the **Received column heading** to sort the messages by date

Figure 3-9: Categories dialog box

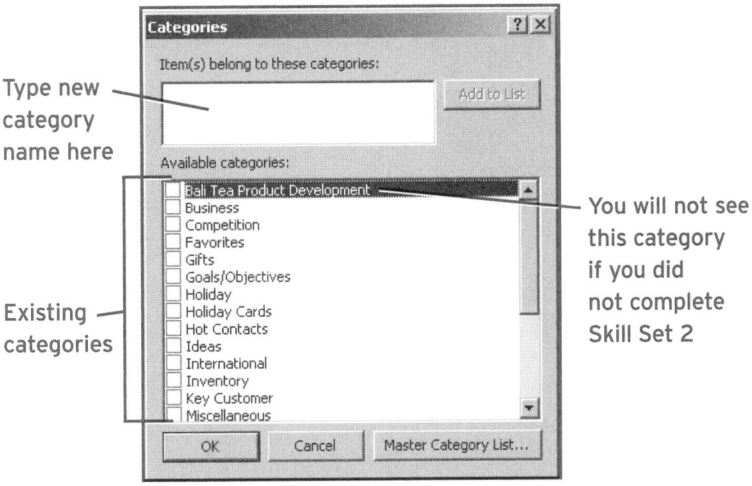

Type new category name here →

Existing → categories

← You will not see this category if you did not complete Skill Set 2

Figure 3-10: Advanced Find dialog box

Selected → category

Messages with Book Signings category assigned to them

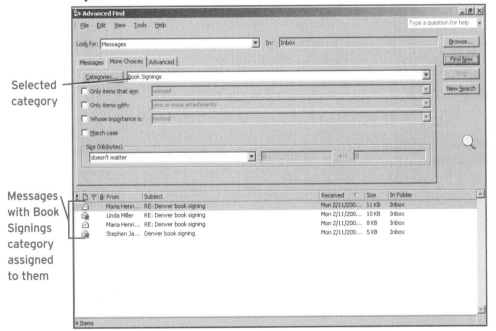

Skill Set 3

Managing Messages

Set Message Options
Modify Message Settings

Unless you specify otherwise, messages you write are sent with default settings indicating a normal level of importance and sensitivity. Sometimes you might want to communicate a higher level of urgency to your recipient or mark a particular message as confidential so the recipient handles it with care. You can change these and other message settings using the Message Options dialog box. You can use this dialog box to set the level of importance and sensitivity, and to include **voting buttons**, which are buttons that appear in the recipients' message form to streamline their response. Voting buttons are useful if you need a quick yes/no or accept/decline response. You can also set delivery options using this dialog box and assign a category to a message.

To add your own voting buttons to a message, click the Use voting buttons check box in the Options dialog box, select the voting button names that appear in the Use voting buttons text box, then type new button names, separating each name with a semicolon.

Activity

1. Click the **Inbox icon** on the Outlook Bar, click the **New Mail Message button**, type **stephenjames@adelphia.net** in the To: box, type your e-mail address in the Cc: box, type **New series** in the Subject box, then press **[Tab]**

2. Type **Do you think we should move forward with the Children's Adventure Guide series?**

3. Click **Options** on the toolbar
   See Figure 3-11.

4. Click the **Importance list arrow**, click **High**, click the **Sensitivity list arrow**, then click **Confidential**

5. Click the **Use voting buttons check box**, click the **Use voting buttons list arrow**, then click **Yes; No**

6. Click the **Request a delivery receipt for this message check box**, click **Close**, then click **Send** on the Message form toolbar

7. Click the **Send/Receive button** on the toolbar, if necessary, then wait until the New series message appears in the Inbox
   When the New series message appears, notice that a red exclamation point indicates this message has a high level of importance.

8. Double-click the **New series message**, compare your screen to Figure 3-12, then click the **Message form Close button**

Figure 3-11: Message Options dialog box

Click to change the level of importance

Click to change Sensitivity setting to Confidential

Click to specify that voting buttons appear in recipients' message form

Click to receive acknowledgment of delivery

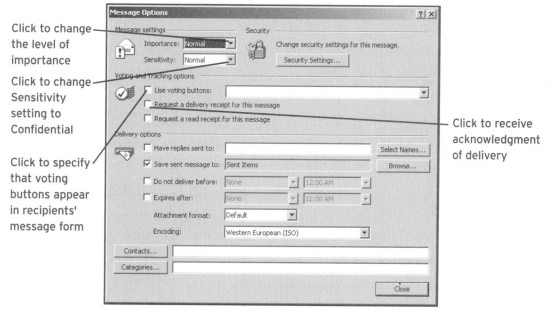

Figure 3-12: Message marked as Confidential with voting buttons

Voting buttons

Yellow banner items indicate message has high importance and is confidential

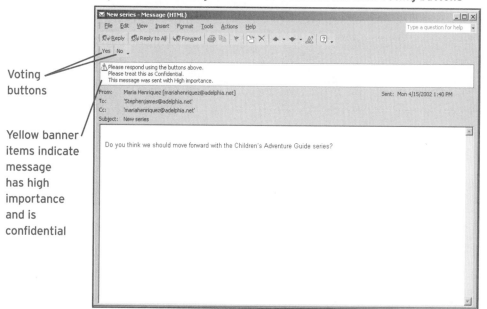

Skill Set 3

Set Message Options
Modify Delivery Options

Sometimes it might be important to have a message delivered according to set specifications. For instance, you might want to choose a window of time when you want a message to be delivered, or to specify that the replies to a certain message be sent to another person. If you are the President of a company, you might send out a message to your employees asking for input on a particular issue. Rather than receiving all the replies yourself, you could specify that replies get sent to your assistant. You set message delivery options using the Delivery options section of the Message Options dialog box.

tip

If you would like to receive a message notifying you that the recipient has opened your message, click the Request a read receipt for this message check box in the Message Options dialog box.

Activity

1. Click the **Inbox icon** on the Outlook Bar, if necessary, then click **the New Mail Message button**

2. Type your e-mail address in the To: box, type **Special Message** in the Subject box, press **[Tab]**, then type **Happy Company Founders' Day!** in the message body

3. Click **Options** on the toolbar to open the Message Options dialog box

4. Click the **Have replies sent to: check box**, then verify that your name appears in the text box

5. Click the **Do not deliver before check box**, then set the date box to the date of your next birthday, and set the time to 8:00 AM
See Figure 3-13.

6. Click **Close**

7. Click **Send**

Figure 3-13: Message Options dialog box with modified delivery options

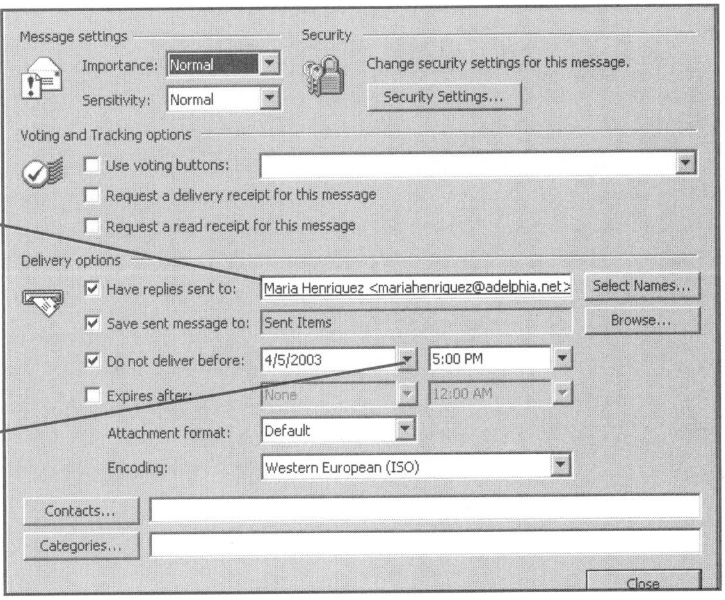

Specify e-mail address of person you want to receive replies

Click to choose delivery date

Message settings	Security
Importance: Normal	Change security settings for this message.
Sensitivity: Normal	Security Settings...

Voting and Tracking options

☐ Use voting buttons:

☐ Request a delivery receipt for this message

☐ Request a read receipt for this message

Delivery options

☑ Have replies sent to: Maria Henriquez <mariahenriquez@adelphia.net>   Select Names...

☑ Save sent message to: Sent Items   Browse...

☑ Do not deliver before: 4/5/2003   5:00 PM

☐ Expires after: None   12:00 AM

Attachment format: Default

Encoding: Western European (ISO)

Contacts...

Categories...

Close

extra!

Setting other message options

In addition to specifying a window of time for delivering a message, you can also set a number of other options in the Message Options dialog box. To set an expiration date for a message, click the Expires after check box, then enter a date in the Expires after text box. To associate a contact with a message, click the Contacts button, then choose a contact name from the list. When you do this, the message will appear as an e-mail item in the Activities tab of the Contact form for that contact. To assign a category to a message, click Categories to open the Categories dialog box, click one or more categories from the list, then click OK.

Skill Set 3

Managing Messages

Set Message Options
Archive Messages Manually

After having an e-mail account for a long time, you might find it helpful to **archive**, or store, your old messages. The Outlook **AutoArchive feature** automatically removes files from your Inbox and other folders that you specify and stores them in an archive file, where they are still accessible but out of the way. By default, AutoArchive is always on. At specific times, it removes old items from folders and places them in the archive file. If you want to archive items from a particular folder earlier or later than the time that is specified for AutoArchive, you can use the Archive dialog box to archive these items manually.

Activity

1. Click the **Inbox icon** [image] on the Outlook Bar, if necessary, click **View** on the menu bar, then click **Folder List**

2. Click the **Inbox folder** in the Folder List, if necessary, click **File** on the menu bar, point to **New**, click **Folder**, type **Travel** in the Name box, click **OK**, then click **No** in the dialog box that appears

3. Drag the **Flight to Los Angeles message** from Linda Miller from the Inbox to the Travel folder in the Folder List, then click the **Travel folder**
   The Travel folder now contains the Flight to Los Angeles message.

4. Click **File** on the menu bar, then click **Archive**
   See Figure 3-14.

5. Click the **Archive items older than list arrow**, then click **Today**

6. Click **OK**
   After a few seconds, the Flight to Los Angeles message is removed from the Travel folder in the Inbox and is placed in a new Travel folder located in the Archive Folders folder.

7. In the Folders list, click the **+ sign** next to Archive Folders, click the **+ sign** next to Inbox, then click the **Travel folder**
   See Figure 3-15.

8. Click the **Inbox icon** [image] on the Outlook Bar, then click the **Folder List Close button**

To change the settings for how your Outlook items are automatically archived, right-click the folder whose AutoArchive settings you want to change, click Properties, click the AutoArchive tab, then specify the time interval that you want for archiving these items.

Figure 3-14: Archive dialog box

Selected folder

Files contained in selected folder will be archived to file specified in this path (yours will be different)

Click to open Calendar to set date

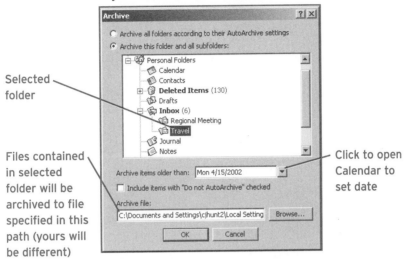

Figure 3-15: Folder List showing archived item

Travel folder that was automatically created, listed under Archive Folders

Travel folder

Message item is now archived

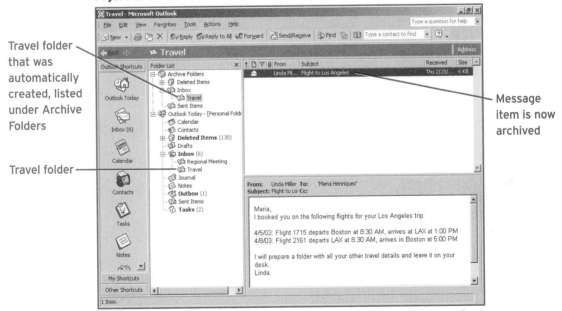

Skill Set 3

Managing Messages

Target Your Skills

1 Use Figure 3-16 as a guide. Write a message to yourself explaining that you just won two tickets for a Carribbean Cruise. Include Yes/No voting buttons, set the Importance level at High, the Sensitivity level to Personal, and specify that replies be sent to you. Send the message, then when you receive it, move it to a new folder you create called Vacation. Finally, save the message first as an .htm file and then as a text file.

Figure 3-16

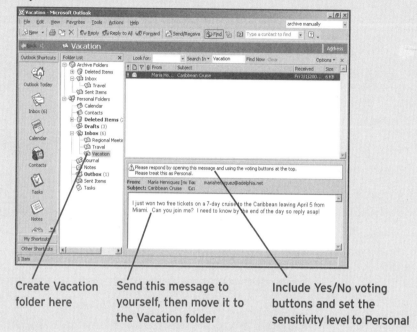

Create Vacation folder here

Send this message to yourself, then move it to the Vacation folder

Include Yes/No voting buttons and set the sensitivity level to Personal

2 Use Figure 3-17 as a guide. Use the Find bar to locate all the messages in your Inbox that have the word cancer in them. Assign a new category to these messages called Cancer Walk. Finally, archive these files.

Figure 3-17

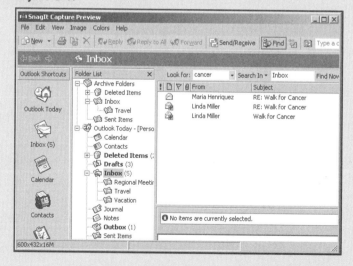

Skill List

1. Create and edit contacts
2. Organize and sort contacts
3. Link contacts to activities and Journal entries

Keeping track of all the people in your work and personal life can be a daunting task and is often more than a paper-based address book or Rolodex can handle. In this skill set, you will learn to use the Contacts component of Outlook to keep track of names, addresses, phone numbers, and other information for the people with whom you interact. You will start by creating new contact entries and editing existing ones. You will then learn ways to organize your contacts by viewing and sorting them in various ways, and grouping them by categories. Finally, you will learn to link other Outlook items to contacts so that you can keep track of the activities associated with a particular contact.

Skill Set 4

Creating and Managing Contacts

Create and Edit Contacts

Add Contacts

You can use the Contacts folder in Outlook to store information about your business associates, friends, and family. In Outlook, a **contact** is a person whose phone numbers, as well as e-mail, home, and business addresses, you want to keep track of. You open the Contacts folder using the Contacts icon on the Outlook Bar. When you first open the Contacts folder, all your contacts appear in **Address Cards view**, which displays a partial listing of each contact's information on what looks like a Rolodex card. To add a new contact, you use the **Contact form**. You use the General tab of the Contact form to enter the name, job title, company, address, phone numbers, and e-mail addresses of a contact. You can use the Details tab to enter additional information about a contact's job as well as personal information such as nickname, birthday, or spouse's name. The other tabs on the Contact form let you keep track of a contact's activities, send an encrypted message to a contact using a digital certificate, and view selected fields about a contact. Table 4-1 describes the Contact form toolbar buttons.

Step 2
You can enter up to three different addresses for a single contact. Click the list arrow next to the Address text box, click Business, Home, or Other to identify the type of address it is, then type the new address. You can add multiple e-mails, phone, and fax numbers as well.

Activity Steps

1. Start Outlook, if necessary, choose your **Profile name**, click **OK**, enter your **password**, then click the **Contacts icon** 📇 on the Outlook Bar
   The Contacts window opens in Address Cards view.

2. Click the **New Contact button** 📇 New ▾ on the toolbar
   The Contact form appears.
   See Figure 4-1.

3. Type **Spencer Hanaway** in the Full Name text box, then press **[Tab]**
   Notice that Hanaway, Spencer automatically appears in the File as box. Outlook will file this name with the last name listed first.

4. Type **Senior Product Manager** in the Job title text box, then press **[Tab]**

5. Type **Tiger Tea Company** in the Company text box, click in the Address text box, type **1445 Pacific Way**, press **[Enter]**, type **San Francisco, CA 94115**, then verify that there is a check mark in the This is the mailing address check box

6. Click in the Business phone text box, type **(415) 555-4563**, click in the E-mail text box, type **spencerhanaway@hotmail.com**, then press **[Tab]**
   The Display as text box shows how the e-mail address will appear.

7. Click the **Details tab**, type **Product Development** in the Department text box, then click **Save and Close** on the toolbar

Figure 4-1: Blank Contact form

Details tab

Type first and last name here

Address text box

Business phone box

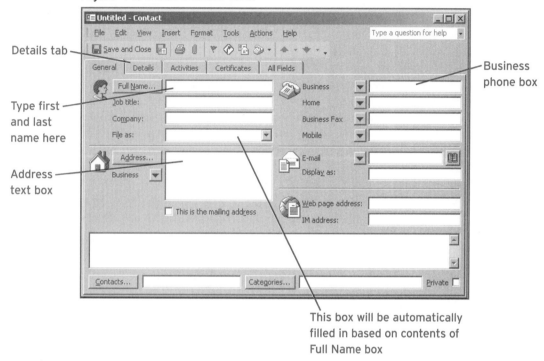

This box will be automatically filled in based on contents of Full Name box

Table 4-1: Contact form toolbar buttons

button	button name	what it does
Save and Close	Save and Close	Saves the current contact and closes the Contact form
	Save and New	Saves the current contact and opens a new, blank Contact form
	Print	Prints all Contact form information for the current contact
	Insert File	Opens the Insert File dialog box, where you select a file to attach to the contact
	Follow Up	Lets you identify a follow-up action and due date for the current contact and adds it to the Calendar
	Display Map of Address	Displays a geographic map of contact's address
	New Message to Contact	Opens the Message form with the current contact's e-mail address in To: box
	AutoDialer	Automatically dials a phone number you select or specify
	Previous Item	Opens a Contact form containing information for the previous contact
	Next Item	Opens a Contact form containing information for the next contact

Skill Set 4
Creating and Managing Contacts

Create and Edit Contacts
Edit Contacts

Because people move, get promoted, get married, and take new jobs, you will likely need to make changes to the contacts in your Contacts folder from time to time. To edit the information for a contact, you need to open the Contact form. You make editing changes just as you would in a word processor such as Word: you select the text you want to change, and then type the new text. You can also use the tools on the toolbar to enhance the information about a contact. For instance, you could attach a photograph of the contact using the Attach File button. You could also use the Follow Up button to insert a reminder to yourself to call, arrange a meeting, or respond to the contact in some way.

To remove a follow up flag, click Clear Flag in the Flag for Follow Up dialog box. When you have completed a follow up action, click the Completed check box.

Activity Steps

1. Click the **Contacts icon**  on the Outlook Bar, if necessary, then double-click the **Riley, Bettijean** address card

2. Click to the left of **Product Manager** in the Job title text box, type **Associate**, then press **[Spacebar]**

3. Click in the Company box, then type **Tiger Tea Company**

4. In the Address section, click the **Business list arrow**, click **Home**, click in the Address box, type **2305 California Street, #3B**, press **[Enter]**, then type **San Francisco, CA 94123**
   See Figure 4-2.

5. Click the **Details tab**, type **Product Development** in the Department box, click in the **Manager's name box**, then type **Spencer Hanaway**

6. Click the **Follow Up button** on the toolbar, click the **Flag to: list arrow**, click **Arrange Meeting**, then click the **first Due by list arrow**
   See Figure 4-3.

7. Click **Today**, click the **second Due by list arrow**, click **5:00 PM**, click **OK**, then click **Save and Close** on the toolbar
   Notice that a Follow Up Flag note appears just below Riley, Bettijean.

Figure 4-2: Edited General tab of Contact form

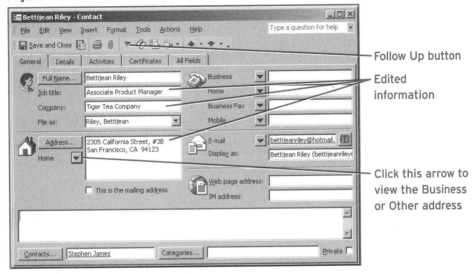

— Follow Up button

Edited information

Click this arrow to view the Business or Other address

Figure 4-3: Flag for Follow Up dialog box

Click to specify type of follow up action

Click when you have completed follow up action

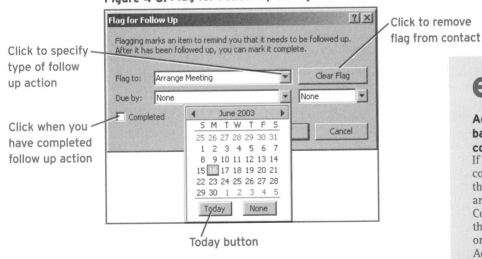

Click to remove flag from contact

Today button

extra!

Adding a contact based on an existing contact

If you need to add a contact who works at the same company as another contact in your Contacts folder, select the address card of the original contact, click Actions on the menu bar, then click New Contact from Same Company. The Contact form opens with the company, address, and phone boxes filled in.

Skill Set 4
Creating and Managing Contacts

Organize and Sort Contacts
Organize Contacts Using Categories

You can organize the contacts in your Contacts folder by assigning different categories to them. A **category** is a word or phrase you use to keep track of items so you can easily find or sort them into related groups. For instance, you might want to assign the VIP category to all the senior executives at your company. Outlook provides a number of predefined categories, from which you can choose, and you can also create your own. You can use the **Ways to Organize pane** to assign new or existing categories to your contacts. You can also assign more than one category to a contact. Once you assign categories to all your contacts, you can view all the contacts in a particular category using By Category view.

To view all the categories assigned to a contact, double-click an address card in Address Cards view, then click Categories to open the Categories dialog box.

Activity Steps

1. Click the **Contacts icon** 📇 on the Outlook Bar, if necessary, then click the **Organize button** 📇 on the toolbar
   The Ways to Organize Contacts pane appears.
   See Figure 4-4.

2. Click **Oakes, Richard**, press and hold **[Ctrl]**, click **Romano, Christina**, release **[Ctrl]**, click the **Add Contacts selected below to list arrow**, scroll down until you see **Key Customer**, click **Key Customer**, then click **Add**

3. Click **Carson, Ridley**, press and hold **[Ctrl]**, click **Hanaway, Spencer**, click **Riley, Bettijean**, then release **[Ctrl]**

4. Click in the **Create a new category called box**, type **Product Development Team**, then click **Create**

5. Click **Add** to assign the Product Development Team category to the three selected contacts

6. Click **View** on the menu bar, point to **Current View**, then click **By Category**
   The two categories you assigned to your contacts appear in a table. You need to expand each category to view its associated contacts.

7. Click the **+ sign** next to Categories: Key Customer (2 items), if necessary, then click the **+ sign** next to Categories: Product Development Team (3 items), if necessary
   All the contacts appear under their assigned categories.
   See Figure 4-5.

8. Click **View** on the menu bar, point to **Current View**, then click **Address Cards**

Figure 4-4: Ways to Organize pane open in Contacts folder

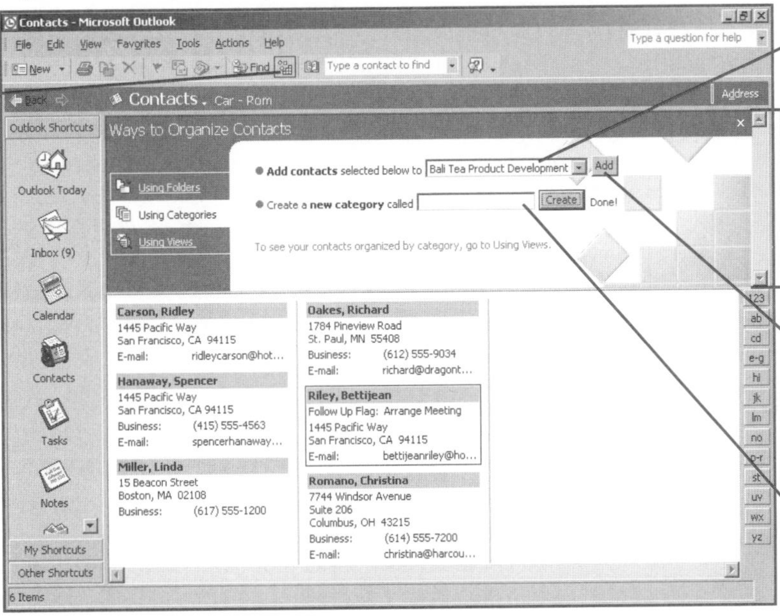

Organize button

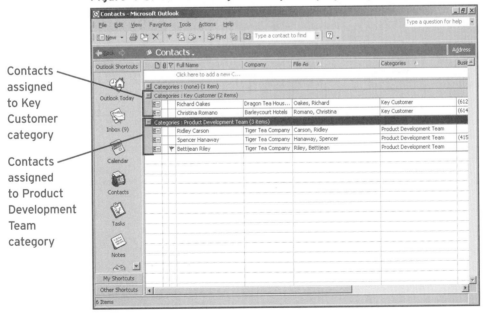

Click to display list of existing categories

Ways to Organize Contacts pane

Click to assign selected category to contact

Type new category name here

Figure 4-5: Contacts organized by category in By Category view

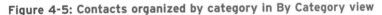

Contacts assigned to Key Customer category

Contacts assigned to Product Development Team category

Skill Set 4
Creating and Managing Contacts

Organize and Sort Contacts

Sort Contacts

The default view for the Contacts folder is Address Cards view. If you have only a few contacts in your Contact list, you will be able to see all of them in this view. However, if you have a lot of contacts and are having trouble finding the one you need, you can use the View menu to switch to a more appropriate view. For instance, if you forget the name of a contact but know that she is employed by Barleycourt Hotels, you can use By Company view to view the contacts by Company. You can use Phone List view to view your contacts in a table. Phone List view is a good view to use if you want to sort your contacts in various ways. You can easily change the sort order in Phone List view by clicking the column heading by which you want to sort. For instance, to sort your contacts by last name in alphabetical order, you click the File As column heading.

To display expanded information for each contact on address cards, click View on the menu bar, point to Current View, then click Detailed Address Cards.

Activity Steps

1. Click the **Contacts icon** on the Outlook Bar, if necessary

2. Click **View** on the menu bar, point to **Current View**, then click **By Company**

   The contacts appear in a table, sorted by company.
   See Figure 4-6.

3. Click **View** on the menu bar, point to **Current View**, then click **Phone List**

   The contacts appear in a table.

4. Click the **Full name column heading**

   The contacts are sorted alphabetically by first names, in ascending order.
   See Figure 4-7.

5. Click the **File As column heading**

   The contacts are now sorted by last names in ascending order.

6. Click the **Company column heading**

   The contacts are now sorted by company names in ascending order.

7. Click **View** on the menu bar, point to **Current View**, then click **Address Cards**

Figure 4-6: Contacts in By Company view

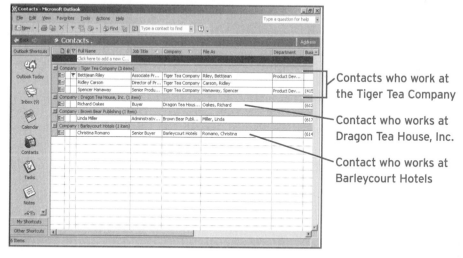

Contacts who work at the Tiger Tea Company

Contact who works at Dragon Tea House, Inc.

Contact who works at Barleycourt Hotels

Figure 4-7: Contacts in Phone List view, sorted by first names

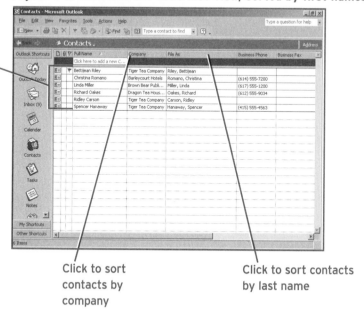

Contacts are sorted by first name

Click to sort contacts by company

Click to sort contacts by last name

extra!

Sorting by more than one field

Sometimes you might want to sort contacts by more than one field. For instance, you might want to sort your contacts first by Company, and then by last name. To do this, click View on the menu bar, point to Current View, then click Customize Current View to open the View Summary dialog box. Click Sort to open the Sort dialog box, specify the fields by which you want to sort (you can choose up to four fields), then click OK twice.

Skill Set 4

Creating and Managing Contacts

Link Contacts to Activities and Journal Entries

Assign Categories to Contacts

If the contacts in your Contacts list are involved in separate aspects of your working or personal life, you can organize them into related groups by assigning categories to them. For instance, you might want to group all your friends into the Personal category, and all your co-workers into the Business category. The activity titled "Organize contacts using Categories" explains how to assign categories to contacts using the Ways to Organize pane. You can also use the Categories dialog box to assign a contact to a category. You can choose from predefined categories or you can create your own.

Step 4
If you did not complete the activity called "Organize Contacts Using Categories," Product Development Team will not appear in the Items belong to these categories text box. In this case, type Direct Reports and ignore the other Step 4 instructions.

Activity Steps

1. Click the **Contacts icon** on the Outlook Bar, if necessary, click **Oakes, Richard**, press and hold **[Ctrl]**, then click **Romano, Christina**

2. Click **Edit** on the menu bar, click **Categories** to open the Categories dialog box, click the **Hot Contacts check box** in the Available categories list, then click **OK**

3. Click **Riley, Bettijean**, right-click to open the shortcut menu, then click **Categories**
   The Categories dialog box opens.

4. Click to the left of **Product Development Team** in the Item(s) belong to these categories box, type **Direct Reports**, type **,** (a comma), then press **[Spacebar]**

5. Click **Add to List**
   Direct Reports appears as a checked item in the Available categories list.
   See Figure 4-8.

6. Click **OK**, click **View** on the menu bar, point to **Current View**, then click **By Category**

7. Click the **+** (plus sign) next to Categories: Direct Reports (1 item), then click the **+** (plus sign) next to Categories: Hot Contacts (2 items)
   The contacts assigned to the Direct Reports category and the Hot Contacts category appear.
   See Figure 4-9.

8. Click **View** on the menu bar, point to **Current View**, then click **Address Cards**

Figure 4-8: Categories dialog box

New category

New category automatically checked

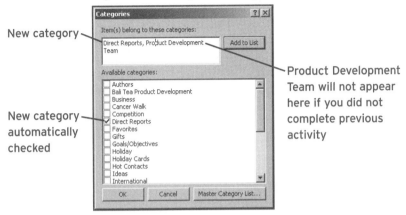

Product Development Team will not appear here if you did not complete previous activity

Figure 4-9: Contacts in By Category view with two new category assignments

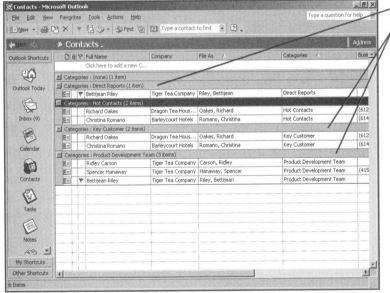

New category

You will not see these categories if you did not complete previous activity

extra!

Removing categories

If you find that you have categories that are no longer relevant, you can remove them. To delete a category, open the Categories dialog box, click Master Category List, click the Category you want to delete, click Delete, then click OK twice. To remove all categories that you have created and revert to the original categories list, open the Categories dialog box, click Master Category List, click Reset, then click OK twice.

Skill Set 4

Creating and Managing Contacts

Link Contacts to Activities and Journal Entries

Track All Activities for Contacts

If you deal with a large number of contacts, you might find it helpful to keep track of the various tasks, appointments, meetings, and conversations associated with each one. You can do this easily in Outlook by linking any item to a contact. For instance, you can link a Calendar appointment, meeting request, or e-mail message to a contact. You can also create Journal items that are linked to a contact. The **Journal** is a folder in Outlook that you can use to store information about activities and interactions with people. For instance, you can create a Journal entry that summarizes a task you completed or a phone conversation you had. Keeping track of such activities is very helpful if you need to show a manager or a client how you have spent your time. You can view all activities associated with a contact in the Activities tab of the Contact form.

Step 3
Be aware that it might take a few seconds for Outlook to find all the activities associated with Richard Oakes.

Activity Steps

1. Click the **Contacts icon** 🔲 on the Outlook Bar, if necessary
2. Double-click the **Richard Oakes address card**
3. Click the **Activities tab** on the Contact form
   All the activities assigned to Richard Oakes appear in a list.
   See Figure 4-10.
4. Double-click the **Bali Tea customer feedback item**
   The Journal Entry form opens, showing the summary of a phone conversation on May 28.
   See Figure 4-11.
5. Click the **Close button** on the Journal Entry form, then double-click the **Dinner meeting item**
   The Dinner meeting-Appointment form opens, showing the details of this Calendar item.
6. Click the **second Start time list arrow**, then click **6:00 PM**
   The meeting start time is now set to 6:00. The meeting end time automatically adjusts to end at 8:00.
7. Click **Save and Close** on the toolbar, then click **Save and Close** on the Richard Oakes-Contact form toolbar

Figure 4-10: Activities tab of Contacts form

Journal entries

Calendar appointments

Phone call Journal entry

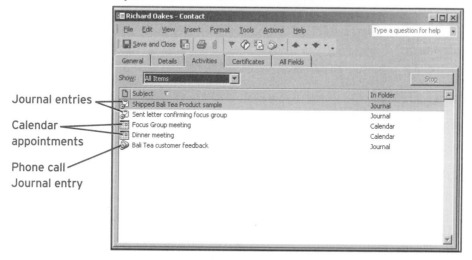

Figure 4-11: Journal Entry form linked to contact

Indicates type of Journal entry

Summary of phone call

Date and time of phone call

Contacts to which this Journal entry is linked appear here

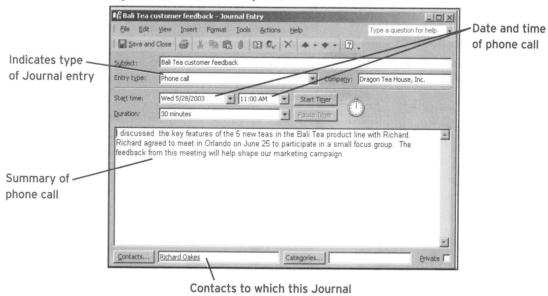

Skill Set 4

Creating and Managing Contacts

Link Contacts to Activities and Journal Entries
Assign Journal Entries to Contacts

If you need to keep track of how you spend your time, then using the Journal is a good idea. For example, you can track your activities to help you write your annual review or to demonstrate to a client how you have billed for your time. You can create **Journal entries** to keep track of any activity, such as summarizing a meeting or a phone call, or sending a contract to a customer. You can also attach files to Journal entries. For instance, you could create a Journal entry about sending a memo and then attach the memo to the Journal entry. You can also record the duration of a Journal entry, either by using a timer or by entering the time yourself. To create a Journal entry, you open the Journal folder and use the New Journal Entry button on the toolbar to open the Journal Entry form. To link a Journal entry to a contact, you use the Select Contacts dialog box. Any Journal entries linked to a contact will appear in the Activities tab of the Contact form for that contact.

By default, your Journal timeline shows seven days. To change the view to a single day, click the Day button on the toolbar. To change the timeline to show a whole month, click the Month button on the toolbar.

Activity Steps

1. Click the **My Shortcuts button** on the Outlook Bar, then click the **Journal icon** [Journal] on the Outlook Bar (If a dialog box opens, click No)

2. Click the **New Journal Entry button** [New ▾] on the toolbar
   The Journal Entry form opens.
   See Figure 4-12.

3. Type **Thank you gift** in the Subject line, press **[Tab]**, click the **Entry type list arrow**, then click **Task**

4. Click in the large text box in the bottom half of the form, then type **Sent Tiger Tea mug set to Richard Oakes and Christina Romano as a thank you gift for participating in focus group.**

5. Click the **Contacts button**
   The Select Contacts dialog box opens.
   See Figure 4-13.

6. Click **Oakes, Richard**, press and hold **[Ctrl]**, click **Romano, Christina**, release **[Ctrl]**, then click **OK**
   Richard Oakes and Christina Romano appear in the Contacts box in the Journal Entry form.

7. Click **Save and Close** on the toolbar, then click the **+ sign** next to Entry Type: Task, if necessary
   The Thank you gift task appears under the current time on the timeline in the Journal window.

8. Click **Outlook Shortcuts** on the Outlook Bar

Figure 4-12: Journal Entry form

Type a subject for your Journal entry here

Click to see a list of available entry types

Click to start a timer which will automatically record the duration of the activity

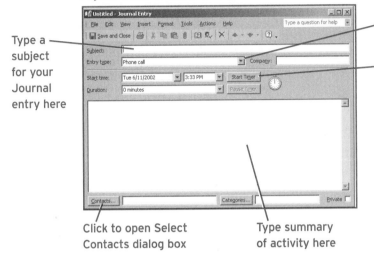

Click to open Select Contacts dialog box

Type summary of activity here

Figure 4-13: Select Contacts dialog box

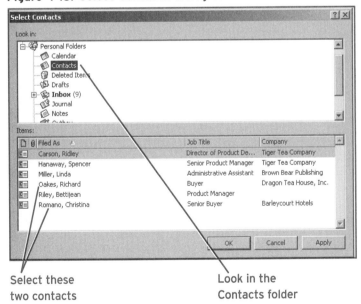

Select these two contacts

Look in the Contacts folder

extra!

Recording items automatically in the Journal

You can set up Outlook so that particular items for certain contacts are automatically recorded. For instance, you can specify that all e-mail messages sent to your boss are automatically recorded as Journal entries. You can also specify that Office XP files be automatically recorded as Journal entries. To do this, click Tools on the menu bar, then click Options to open the Options dialog box. Click Journal Options to open the Journal Options dialog box, specify which items or types of Office files you want the Journal to record and for which contacts, then click OK twice.

Skill Set 4

Creating and Managing Contacts

Target Your Skills

1 Use Figure 4-14 as a guide. Add the four contacts shown. Edit the Carson Lawrence contact form to change the company to Looking Good Times, Inc. and change the address, phone number, and e-mail entries with information you make up. Assign the Hot Contacts category to Carson Lawrence and Marcia Hammond. Assign a new category called Sales Team to Marianne O'Neill and Roxanne Waters. Sort the contacts in Phone List view by Company.

Figure 4-14

Hammond, Marcia		O'Neill, Marianne	
Full Name:	Marcia Hammond	Full Name:	Marianne O'Neill
Job Title:	Buyer	Job Title:	Sales Manager
Company:	Knock Out Beauty Supply	Company:	All Natural Cosmetics, Inc.
Business:	1414 Oakwood Drive Rockville, MD 20850	Business:	6200 Lakeview Drive Houston, TX 77008
Business:	(301) 555-3200	Business:	(713) 555-2300
E-mail:	marcia@knockoutbeauty.com	E-mail:	marianne@naturalcosmetics.com
Categories:	Hot Contacts	Categories:	Sales Team

Lawrence, Carson		Waters, Roxanne	
Full Name:	Carson Lawrence	Full Name:	Roxanne Waters
Job Title:	Columnist	Job Title:	Vice President, Sales and Marketing
Company:	Beauty Tips Newsletter	Company:	All Natural Cosmetics, Inc.
Business:	15672 N.E. 29th Place Suite 404 Bellevue, WA 98007	Department:	Sales
		Business:	6200 Lakeview Drive Houston, TX 77008
Business:	(425) 555-9876	Business:	(713) 555-2300
E-mail:	carson@beautytips.com	E-mail:	roxanne@naturalcosmetics.com
Categories:	Hot Contacts	Categories:	Sales Team

2 Use Figure 4-15 as a guide. Create a new contact for Melanie Wu. Melanie has signed up for a Day of Beauty at the Better Living Spa, where you work. Add the six appointments shown in the list (pick your own day and times). Then add the two Journal entries shown, making up your own information. Link Melanie Wu to each item. View all the items in the Activities tab as shown.

Figure 4-15

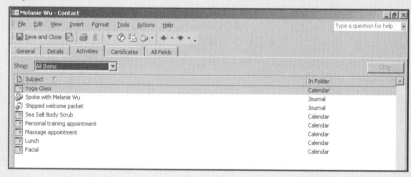

Skill List

1. Create and update tasks
2. Modify task organization and Task view
3. Accept, decline, or delegate tasks
4. Create and modify notes
5. Use categories to manage tasks and notes

If you are a busy person, you probably need a system to help keep track of all the tasks you need to accomplish. You could keep track of such tasks using an old fashioned to-do list. However, you can also take advantage of the powerful task-management features of Outlook. In this skill set, you will learn to use the Tasks component of Outlook to keep track of the tasks that you need to complete. You will create and update tasks, assign tasks to other people, and respond to task requests sent to you by others. You will also learn to use the Notes component of Outlook to record your thoughts and ideas. You will learn how to create, edit, and organize notes, as well as how to associate a note with a contact.

Skill Set 5

Creating and Managing Tasks and Notes

Create and Update Tasks

Create Tasks

You can use the Tasks folder in Outlook to keep track of **tasks**, which are errands or activities you need to perform and that you can track through their completion. By default, tasks appear in Simple List view in the Tasks window, which displays tasks in a grid format showing the completion status, subject, and due date for each task. To create a new task, you use the **Task form**, which contains two tabs. You use the Task tab to enter basic information, such as the subject, due date, and start date of the task. You can also use the Task tab to indicate the completion status and completion percentage, set a priority level, and enter descriptive information about the task. You use the Details tab of the Task form to indicate the completion date of the task, and enter information about the number of hours it took to complete the task. You use the Save and Close button to save new tasks to the Tasks folder. You can use the Delete button on the toolbar to delete a task.

Activity

To enter a new task quickly in Simple List view, click Click here to add a new task at the top of the grid, type the subject for the new task, enter a due date, then press [Enter].

1. Start Outlook, if necessary, choose your Profile name, click **OK**, enter your password, then click the **Tasks icon** on the Outlook Bar
   The contents of the Tasks folder appear in Simple List view.

2. Click the **New Task button** New on the toolbar
   The Task form appears.
   See Figure 5-1.

3. Type **Write memo to Steve James** in the Subject text box

4. Click the **Due date list arrow**, click the date for tomorrow, click the **Start date list arrow**, then click **Today**

5. Click the **Status list arrow**, then click **In Progress**

6. Click the large text box below the Reminder check box, then type **Summarize feedback on marketing plan for Brown Bear Adventure Guides.**, then click the **Save and Close button** on the toolbar
   The new task appears as an item in Simple list view.
   See Figure 5-2.

7. Click the **Write memo to Steve James** task, then click the **Delete button** on the toolbar
   The task is deleted from the Tasks folder.

Figure 5-1: Task form

Type task title here

Type details about task here

Click to set due date

Click to set start date

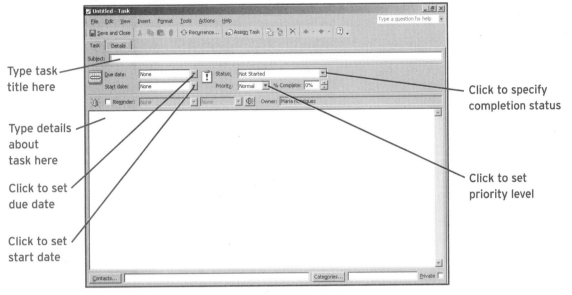

Click to specify completion status

Click to set priority level

Figure 5-2: New task in Tasks folder in Simple List view

Delete button

New task

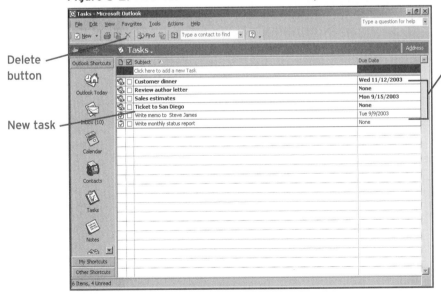

Your list may be different

extra!

Viewing tasks on the TaskPad

Saved tasks appear in the Tasks window and also on the TaskPad. The **TaskPad** is a small window that shows a list of tasks and appears in the Calendar window. By default, the TaskPad shows tasks that are active for the current day.

Skill Set 5

Creating and Managing Tasks and Notes

Create and Update Tasks
Update Tasks

Once in a while, you will probably need to make changes to tasks to update them. For instance, you might need to change the priority level of a task from low to high, or move a due date earlier or later. To make changes to a task, you open the Task form and make edits just as you would in a word processor. You also might have some tasks that recur at certain intervals. For instance, perhaps you need to write a weekly status report for your boss. Instead of manually creating a new task every week, you can update a task so that it recurs. A **recurring task** is a task that occurs repeatedly at regular intervals. You use the Task Recurrence dialog box to specify a recurrence pattern for a task.

Step 5
You can also open the Recurrence dialog box by clicking Actions on the Task form menu bar, then clicking Recurrence.

Activity

1. Click the **Tasks icon** on the Outlook Bar, if necessary, then double-click **Write monthly status report**

2. Click the **Due date list arrow**, then click the date for tomorrow

3. Click the **Status list arrow**, then click **In Progress**, then click the **% Complete up arrow** three times to change the setting to **75%**

4. Click the **Priority list arrow**, then click **High**
   See Figure 5-3.

5. Click the **Recurrence button** on the toolbar
   The Task Recurrence dialog box opens.
   See Figure 5-4.

6. Click the **Monthly option button**, click the **Regenerate new task 1 month(s) after each task is completed option button**, then click **OK**

7. Click the **Save and Close button** on the Task form toolbar

Figure 5-3: Edited task in Task form

Recurrence button —

Click to change due date to tomorrow

Click to change start date to today

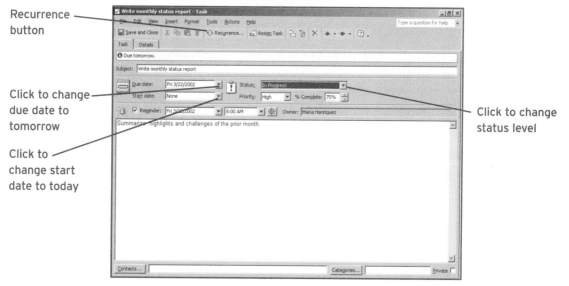

Click to change status level

Figure 5-4: Task Recurrence dialog box

Monthly option button

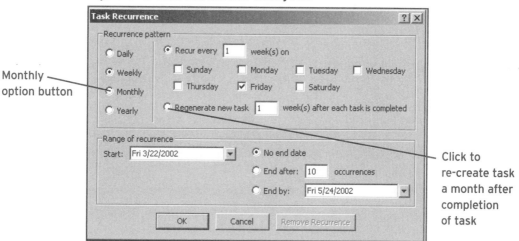

Click to re-create task a month after completion of task

Skill Set 5

Creating and Managing Tasks and Notes

Modify Task Organization and Task View
Assign Tasks to One or More Contacts

If you have administrative resources at your disposal, you might have the luxury of assigning the tasks in your task list to someone else to handle. You can assign a task to someone else by using the New Task Request command. When you use the New Task Request command, the Task form opens and contains a To: text box, where you can type the name of the contact to whom you want to assign the task. You use the Task form to complete the detailed information about the task, such as start date, due date, and priority level, and then you use the Send button on the toolbar to send the task request to the assigned person. The assigned person receives the task request as an e-mail message in their Inbox and can then accept, decline, or delegate the task. When you assign a task to someone else, the task still appears in your task folder. When the assigned person accepts your task, the task will show the assigned person as the task owner.

You can view additional task details in Simple List view by opening the Preview pane. To do this, click View on the menu bar, then click Preview Pane. To close the Preview pane, click View on the menu bar, then click Preview Pane again.

Activity

1. Click the **Tasks icon** on the Outlook Bar, if necessary, click the **New list arrow** on the toolbar, then click **Task Request**
   The Task form appears.

2. Click the **To: button**
   The Select Task Recipient dialog box opens.
   See Figure 5-5.

3. Click **Linda Miller** in the Name list, click **To**, then click **OK**
   Linda Miller appears in the To: box in the Task form.

4. Press **[Tab]** twice, then type **Handouts for Editorial Month-in-Review meeting** in the Subject box

5. Click the **Due date list arrow**, click the date for tomorrow, click the **Start date list arrow**, then click the date for tomorrow

6. Verify that both check boxes below the Start date list box are checked

7. Click in the large text box at the bottom of the form, then type **Please make 25 copies of my presentation for tomorrow's meeting.**
   See Figure 5-6.

8. Click the **Send button**

Figure 5-5: Select Task Recipient dialog box

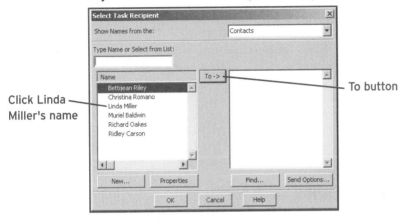

Click Linda
Miller's name

To button

Figure 5-6: Completed Task Request form

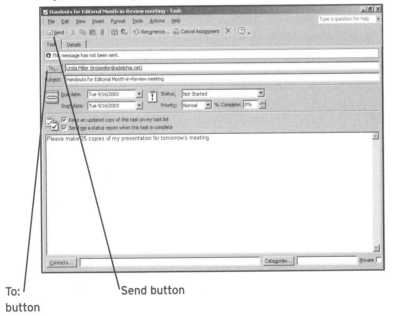

To:
button

Send button

extra!

Viewing and sorting tasks

If you find yourself getting overwhelmed by a huge number of tasks, you can organize your tasks by sorting and viewing them in different ways. You use the commands on the Current View menu to specify how to view your task list. For example, to view only the tasks that are due in the next week, click View on the menu bar, point to Current View, then click Next Seven Days. Some of the other views available on the Current View menu include Detailed List, which shows most of the details for each task in a grid format; Overdue Tasks, which shows only those tasks whose due date has passed; and Assignment, which shows all the tasks you've assigned to others. You can also sort your tasks quickly in any view by clicking the column heading by which you want to sort. For instance, to sort your tasks by the date they are due, click the Due Date column heading in Simple List view.

Skill Set 5

Creating and Managing Tasks and Notes

Accept, Decline, or Delegate Tasks

Accept Tasks

Just as you can assign tasks to other people to complete, you can also receive task assignments from others. You receive task requests from others in the form of e-mail messages delivered to your Inbox. If you agree to take ownership of the task, you can use the Accept button on the toolbar to send a message to the task sender informing them that you agree to see the task through to completion. You can provide a personalized message to the sender, or you can simply send a generic acceptance. If you send a personalized message, you can also attach a file. For instance, if a task request asks you to provide or prepare a particular file, you can attach the requested file to your acceptance message. Tasks for which you accept ownership are added to your Tasks folder.

tip

To view only the tasks you have completed, click View on the menu bar, point to Current View, then click Completed Tasks. To view only tasks you have not yet completed, click View on the menu bar, point to Current View, then click Active Tasks.

Activity

1. Click the **Inbox icon** on the Outlook Bar

2. Click the **From column heading** to sort the messages by sender, then double-click the message **Task Request: Sales estimates from Stephen James**
   The Sales estimates-Task form opens.
   See Figure 5-7.

3. Click the **Accept button** ✓ Accept on the toolbar
   The Task Request: Sales estimates message disappears from your screen and the next message in your Inbox appears.

4. Click the **Task Form Close button,** then Click the **Tasks icon** on the Outlook Bar
   The Sales estimates task now appears in the Tasks folder.

5. Click the **check box** to the left of Sales estimates
   A strikethrough appears over the Sales estimates item, indicating that you have completed this task.
   See Figure 5-8.

6. Click the **Delete button** ☒

Figure 5-7: Task form with task request

Accept button

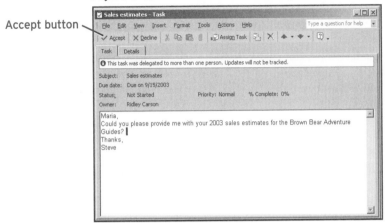

Figure 5-8: Completed task in Simple List view

Check mark in box and strikethrough text indicate task is completed

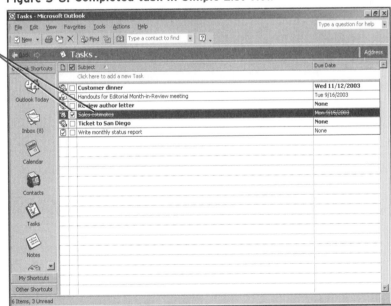

Skill Set 5

Creating and Managing Tasks and Notes

Accept, Decline, or Delegate Tasks
Decline Tasks

If you are a particularly capable person, others who appreciate your ability to get things done will probably send you task requests once in a while. For any number of reasons, you might need to decline a task request. You decline a task request using the Decline button on the Task form toolbar. You can choose to send a generic decline message, or you can send a personalized message to the requester that explains your reasons for rejecting the task request. Task requests that you decline do not get saved to your Tasks folder.

tip

You can also accept and decline tasks when your Inbox is in Messages view. To do this, click the Accept or Decline buttons in the Preview pane.

Activity

1. Click the Inbox icon ▧ on the Outlook Bar

2. Click the **From column heading** to sort the messages by sender, then scroll so you can see the messages from Linda Miller
   See Figure 5-9.

3. Double-click the message **Task Request: Review author letter** from Linda Miller
   See Figure 5-10.

4. Click the **Decline button**
   The Task Request: Review author letter message automatically closes. The task request disappears from your screen.

5. Click the **Message Window Close button**, then click the **Tasks icon** ▧ on the Outlook Bar
   The Review author letter task does not appear in your Tasks folder because you declined it.

Figure 5-9: Inbox sorted by sender

Click to sort
messages
by sender

Double-click
this message

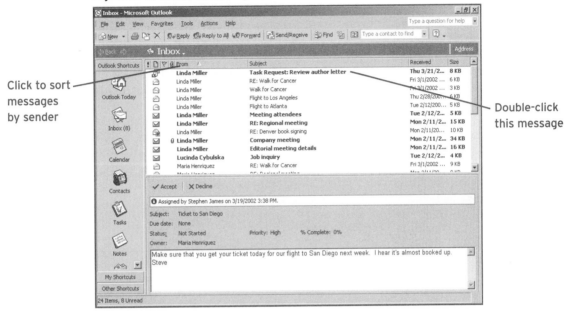

Figure 5-10: Task Request form

Decline
button

You might see
a different
message here

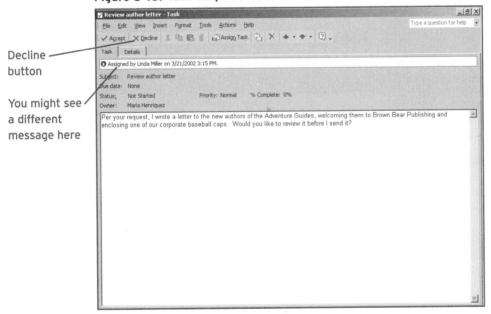

Skill Set 5

Creating and Managing Tasks and Notes

Accept, Decline, or Delegate Tasks
Delegate Tasks

Sometimes you might receive task requests that would be more appropriate for another person to handle. In such cases, you can delegate a task request to someone else. To delegate a task, you use the Assign Task button to open the Task form. You specify the name of the person to whom you want to assign the task, then use the Send button to send it to them. When you assign a task request to another person, a message is sent to the original requester that provides an update on the task. The task also is saved to your Tasks folder. Once you assign a task to someone, his or her name will appear as the temporary owner of the task. If the person to whom you assigned the task accepts the task, then that person becomes the permanent owner of the task. If he or she declines the task, then the task is returned to you and your name appears as the owner of the task.

The owner of a task is the only person who can make changes to the task. When the owner of a task makes changes to it, all copies of the task get updated.

Activity

1. Click the **Inbox icon** 🔄 on the Outlook Bar

2. Click the **From column heading** to sort the messages by sender, if necessary, then scroll so you can see the messages from Stephen James

3. Double-click the **Task Request: Ticket to San Diego** message from Stephen James
   The Ticket to San Diego - Task form opens.

4. Click the **Assign Task button** 🗇 Assign Task on the toolbar
   A To: text box appears in the Task Request form. *See Figure 5-11.*

5. Click the **To: button** to open the Select Task Recipient dialog box, double-click **Linda Miller** in the Name list, then click **OK**
   Linda Miller appears in the To: box.

6. Click at the top of the large text box at the bottom of the form, type **Please book me a ticket to San Diego on that flight we discussed yesterday.**, then click the **Send button** 📧 Send on the toolbar

7. Click the **Tasks icon** 📋 on the Outlook Bar, then double-click the **Ticket to San Diego task**
   The Task form opens showing that Linda Miller now is the owner of this task and that she has not yet responded to your task request. *See Figure 5-12.*

8. Click the **Delete button** ✕ on the toolbar, then click the **Task form close button**

Figure 5-11: Task Request form with empty To: box for delegating to another person

Send button ——

To: button —

You might see a different message here

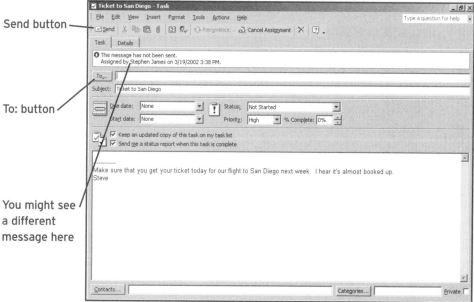

Figure 5-12: Task form showing Linda Miller as the task owner

Indicates Linda Miller has not yet responded to the task request (your message may be different)

Indicates Linda Miller is owner of this task

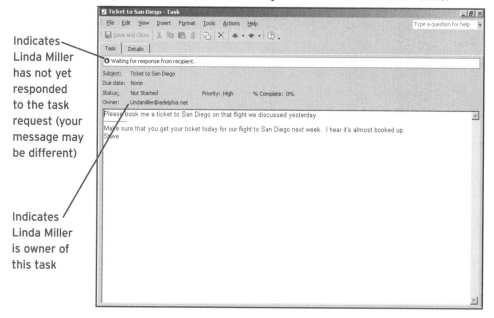

Skill Set 5

Creating and Managing Tasks and Notes

Create and Modify Notes
Create and Edit Notes

If you are the kind of person who jots down information about various things on sticky notes and posts them around your work area, then you will love the Notes feature of Outlook. Notes are computerized sticky notes that you can place anywhere on your screen. You can use Notes to write reminders, notes to yourself, inspirational words of wisdom, or anything you want. You use the **Note form** to write a new note. You use the Close button on the Note form to close the Note form and save a note to your Notes folder.

To change the default color, size, and font used for notes, click Tools on the menu bar, then click Options to open the Options dialog box. Click Note Options on the Preferences tab, make your selections for color, size and font, and then click OK.

Activity

1. Click the **Notes icon** [icon] on the Outlook Bar

2. Click the **New Note button** [New button] on the toolbar
   A new note form appears with the date and time at the bottom. *See Figure 5-13.*

3. Type **Buy flowers and card today for Linda's birthday lunch**, then click the **Note Form Close button**
   The Note appears as an icon in the Notes folder. *See Figure 5-14.*

4. Double-click the **Buy flowers and card today for Linda's birthday lunch note**

5. Click to the right of lunch in the Note form, press **[Enter]**, type **Make reservation for 8 at Lillian's for 12:00**, then click the **Note form Close button**
   The changes are saved to the note.

Figure 5-13: Blank Note form

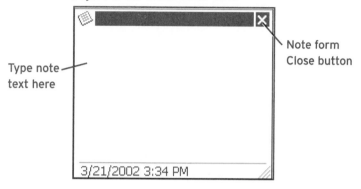

Type note text here

Note form Close button

3/21/2002 3:34 PM

Figure 5-14: Notes folder with new note

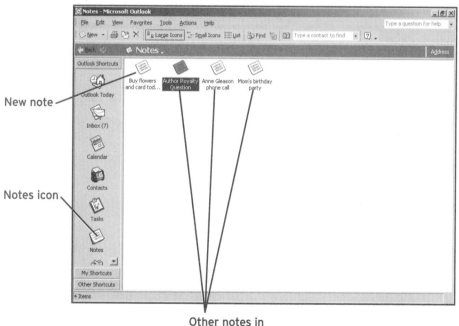

New note

Notes icon

Other notes in Notes folder

Skill Set 5

Creating and Managing Tasks and Notes

Create and Modify Notes
Assign Contacts to Notes

If you use the Notes feature frequently, your Notes folder will fill up fast with a large number of notes. Finding a particular note when your Notes folder is over-flowing with notes can be frustrating and time-consuming. One way to help you retrieve the notes you need is to associate each note with a particular person from your Contacts folder. For instance, perhaps you created a note during a phone call with your boss that contains critical information. So that you can quickly retrieve this note, you can link the note to your boss's name in your Contacts folder. When you need to locate the note again, you can open the Activities tab of your boss's Contact form and view all notes that are linked to your boss. To assign a contact to a Note, you use the Contacts command on the Note form menu. You open the Note form menu by using the menu button located in the upper-left corner of the Note form.

To forward a note to a contact, click the Note form menu button, click Forward, type the e-mail address of the person to whom you want to forward the note in the To: box, then click Send.

Activity

1. Click the **Notes icon** 🖼 on the Outlook Bar, if necessary, then click the **New Note button** on the toolbar

2. Type **Editorial Summer Outing**, then press **[Enter]**

3. Type **Ask Linda to plan day of fun for editorial team**

4. Click the **menu button** 🔲 in the upper-left corner of the Note form
   The Note form menu opens.
   See Figure 5-15.

5. Click **Contacts**
   The Contacts for Note dialog box opens.
   See Figure 5-16.

6. Click **Contacts, click Miller, Linda** in the Items list, click **OK,** click **Close** in the Contacts for Note dialog box, then click the **Note form Close button**

7. Click the **Contacts icon** 🔲 on the Outlook Bar, double-click the **Miller, Linda address card** to open the Linda Miller Contact form, click the **Activities tab,** click the **Show list arrow,** then click **Notes**
   The Editorial Summer Outing Note appears, indicating this note is linked to Linda Miller.

8. Click the **Contact form Close button**

Figure 5-15: Note form menu

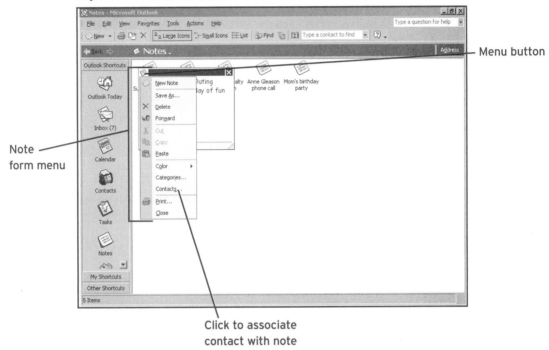

Menu button

Note
form menu

Click to associate
contact with note

Figure 5-16: Contacts for Note dialog box

Click to
select contact
from list

Skill Set 5

Creating and Managing Tasks and Notes

Use Categories to Manage Tasks and Notes
Assign Categories to Notes

If you use the Notes feature frequently, you will need to develop a system to keep your notes organized. Otherwise, you run the risk of accumulating hundreds of "unclassified" notes in your Notes folder, making it extremely difficult to find the one you want. To help keep your notes organized, you can assign categories to your notes so that you can look at related notes together. You can assign any of Outlook's predefined categories, or create new categories of your own. Once you assign categories to your notes, you can use By Category view to view the notes within each category. You assign categories to notes using the Categories command on the Note form menu.

Activity

Step 2
You can also assign categories to tasks. To do this, open the Task form for the task you want to categorize, click the Categories button, specify the category you want to assign, then click OK.

1. Click the **Notes icon** 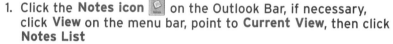 on the Outlook Bar, if necessary, click **View** on the menu bar, point to **Current View**, then click **Notes List**
   The contents of your Notes folder appear in a list format. *See Figure 5-17.*

2. Double-click the **Mom's birthday party note**, click the **menu button**, then click **Categories**
   The Categories dialog box opens.

3. Scroll down, click the **Personal check box** in the Available categories list, click **OK**, then click the **Note form Close button**

4. Click the **Author Royalty Question note**, press and hold [Ctrl], click the **Anne Gleason phone call note**, release [Ctrl], click **Edit** on the menu bar, then click **Categories**

5. Click in the **Item(s) belong to these categories box**, type **Authors**, click **Add to List**, then click **OK**

6. Click **View** on the menu bar, point to **Current View**, then click **By Category**
   The Categories you assigned to your notes appear. *See Figure 5-18.*

7. Click the **plus sign (+)** next to Categories: Authors (2 items), then click **(+)** next to Categories: Personal (1 item)
   The notes appear under their assigned categories.

Figure 5-17: Contents of Notes folder in Notes List view

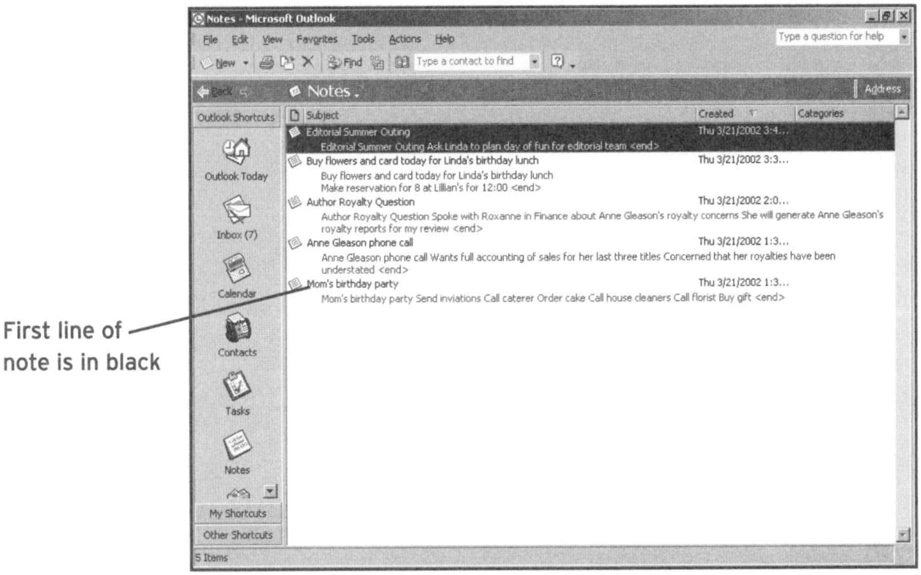

First line of
note is in black

Figure 5-18: Contents of Notes folder in By Categories view

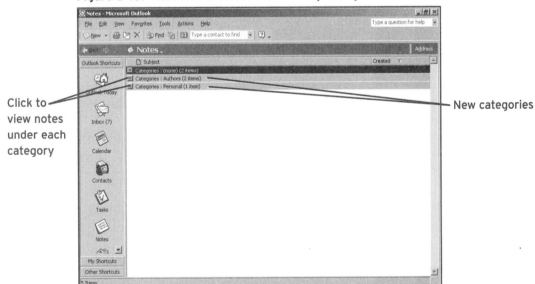

Click to
view notes
under each
category

New categories

Skill Set 5

Creating and Managing Tasks and Notes

Target Your Skills

1 Create the tasks and note shown in Figure 5-19. Update the Finalize agenda task so that it shows a due date of tomorrow, and change its priority level to High. Create a new category called Spring Conference and assign it to the note and the tasks shown in the grid. Assign the Book airlines task and the Order luggage tags note to a contact in your Contacts folder. (Assign Linda Miller if you don't have any contacts of your own.)

2 Open the Task Request: Customer dinner message from Ridley Carson in your Inbox. Assign the task to Bettijean Riley, providing the information shown in Figure 5-20, then send the task request.

Figure 5-19

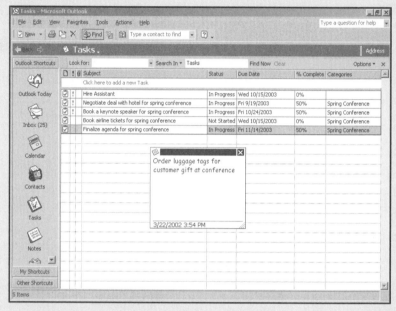

Figure 5-20

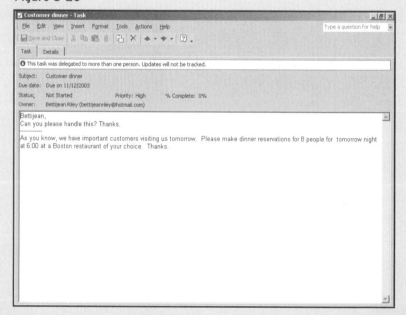

Projects List

Project 1 – E-mail Messages for Vision Productions

Project 2 – Meeting Schedules for Pacific Imports

Project 3 – Message Management for Career Corner

Project 4 – Contact Management for Paradise Realty

Project 5 – Tasks and Notes for Step One Consulting

The Outlook Core skill sets cover a broad range of e-mail and scheduling tasks—from organizing meetings, appointments, and contacts to managing e-mail efficiently. In the following projects, you will use Outlook to create and view e-mail messages, schedule meetings and appointments, manage e-mail messages, create and manage contacts, and work with tasks and notes.

Project for Skill Set 1

Creating and Viewing Messages

E-mail Messages for Vision Productions

As the Office Manager of Vision Productions, located in San Diego, California, your job is to coordinate the activities of the filmmakers involved in shooting a new documentary on the life and work of the artist Michelangelo. The documentary will be set in various locations throughout Italy, and will also involve an Italian film production company based in Florence. In this project, you will receive, read, and send messages to set up meetings between the filmmakers from the home office in San Diego and those from the Italian production company in Florence.

1. Open and read the **Florence shooting schedule message** from Enrico Mazzini, open and print the Word document called **Florence Shooting Schedule.doc** that accompanies the message as an attachment, close the document, then forward the message to yourself

2. Open and read the **Travel Itinerary message** from Mina Harrison, print the e-mail in Memo style over two pages with 1" margins on all four sides of the page, then close the message

3. Open and read the **Hotel in Florence message** from Enrico Mazzini, then add Enrico Mazzini as a new contact to your address book

4. Reply to the message with the text shown in Figure OP 1-1

5. Compose and send an e-mail to Mina Harrison at **minaharrison@hotmail.com** with the subject **Reservations** and the text **I've made the reservations. The hotel will e-mail a confirmation directly.**

6. Create a signature for Mina Harrison that appears as shown in Figure OP 1-2

7. Compose and send an e-mail to Enrico Mazzini at enricomazzini@hotmail.com that includes Revised Itinerary as the subject and the text **Here is a revised version of the travel itinerary.**, attaches the file **Revised Travel Itinerary.doc**, and uses the signature you just created for Mina Harrison

8. Change the Inbox view to view only Sent messages, then customize the view to change the grid line style to **Solid** and the grid line color to **bright blue**

9. Reset the view to the default setting, then remove the signature for Mina Harrison

Figure OP 1-1: Reply message

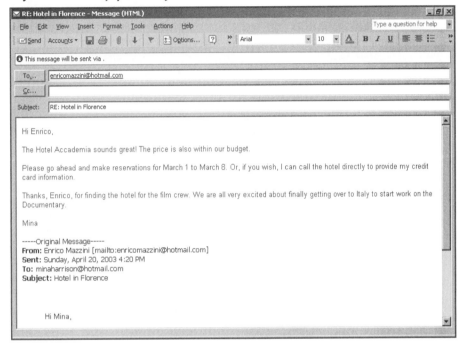

Figure OP 1-2: Signature for Mina Harrison

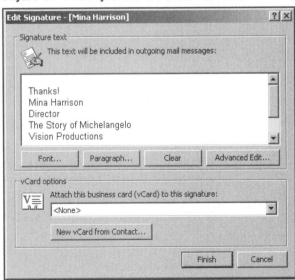

Project for Skill Set 2

Scheduling

Meeting Schedules for Pacific Imports

Pacific Imports is a small retail outlet based in Seattle, Washington, that sells craft products from various Pacific Rim nations such as Japan, Malaysia, Australia, Chile, and Mexico. Meetings are held frequently to discuss new products and to plan marketing strategies. In this project, you will use Outlook to add appointments to the Calendar, schedule meetings and resources, and manage meeting requests for two managers at Pacific Imports: Derek Thirlwell and Shaun Richter, and for Rie Nishimura, who is in charge of Resources.

1. In the Calendar, enter the appointment **Planning Meeting** at **3:00 pm** for tomorrow; the meeting will last **2 hours** and take place in the **Coral Reef Conference Room**

2. Create a new category called **Planning**, add the Planning meeting to the Planning category, make the meeting one that recurs every month on the same day (e.g., the first Tuesday), save and close the meeting, then apply a conditional format to the Planning Meeting that makes it a **Business** meeting based on the condition that **planning** appears in the subject

3. Schedule an all-day event for next Wednesday called **Employee Appreciation Day** that will take place at **Mayfair Roller Rink**; remove the reminder, show the time as **Out of Office**, label the meeting as **Must Attend**, include the text shown in Figure OP 2-1, then save and close the event

4. Schedule a meeting from **10:00** to **12:00** in the **Pacific Oasis Conference Room** on another free day in your calendar that uses **Rei Nishimura** as the Resource and discusses **Taiwan Imports**, with **Derek Thirlwell** and **Shaun Richter** as required attendees

5. In your Inbox, open the **Product Launch Meeting message**, accept the meeting request, edit the response by adding the message as shown in Figure OP 2-2, send a copy of the message to **Derek Thirlwell** and a copy to yourself, then view the meeting date in the calendar

6. Open the **New Zealand Conference message** in your inbox, decline the meeting request with the message **I'm sorry, Derek. I need to be in Taiwan that week.**, open the **Australia Manager Meeting message**, propose a new meeting time of **1:00 pm** to **2:30 pm**, then send a copy of the message to yourself

7. Print all the appointments in the **Daily Style** for **April 3, 2003**

Figure OP 2-1: All-day event scheduled

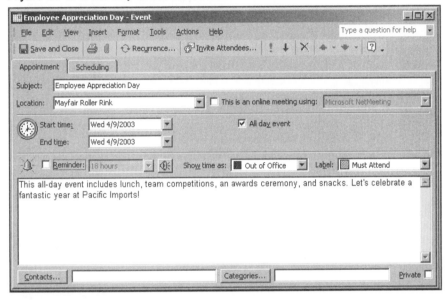

Figure OP 2-2: Reply to Product Launch meeting request

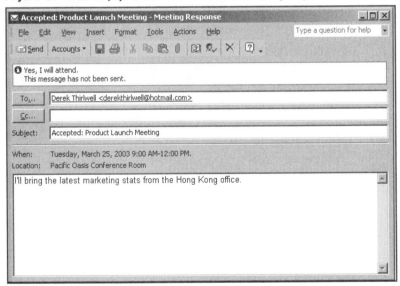

Project for Skill Set 3

Managing Messages

Message Management for Career Corner

Career Corner is an employment agency that finds jobs for people with business administrative skills and provides a variety of career counseling services. The company also maintains an active Web site. As the Administrative Assistant, you use Outlook to manage the many e-mails received from job hunters who browse the Web site. You need to develop an effective system for managing these messages. In this project, you will create a system for managing messages related to positions for Account Managers.

1. Use the Find feature to find all messages in the Inbox that contain **Account Manager** in the Subject line
   You should find three messages containing Account Manager in the Subject line.

2. Select the following messages: **Account Manager Position Available**, **Account Manager: Regional**, and **Account Managers Needed**

3. Create a new folder in the Inbox called **Account Manager Positions** but do not add a shortcut to the Outlook Bar, then move the selected messages into the new folder

4. Open the **Account Manager Position Available message** from the Account Manager Positions folder, save the message as a Text Only (*.txt) file in the location in which your store your project files, then open the file in Notepad
   The file appears in Notepad as shown in Figure OP 3-1.

5. Open the **Account Managers Needed message**, save it as an HTML file in the location in which you store your project files, then view the file in Internet Explorer

6. Assign all messages in the Account Manager Positions folder to a new category called **Seattle Postings**, then use the Advanced Find feature to display the messages you have assigned to the Seattle Postings category
   The messages appear in the Seattle Postings category as shown in Figure OP 3-2.

7. Send an **Important** and **Confidential** message to Nathan Chang at *nathanchang@hotmail.com* with the subject **New Positions** and the text **Can we meet at 2 pm to discuss the new Account Manager positions?** that uses the voting buttons for a Yes/No response and requests a read receipt for the message

8. Open the Account Manager Positions folder, then modify the AutoArchive properties so that the folder is archived in one week

Figure OP 3-1: Text only file shown in Notepad

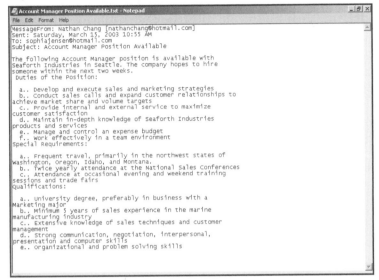

Figure OP 3-2: Messages in Seattle Postings category

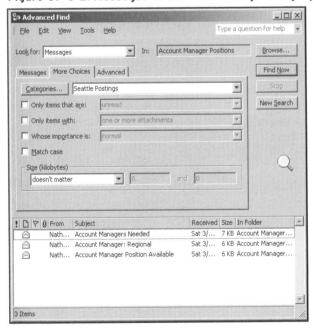

Project for Skill Set 4

Creating and Managing Contacts

Contact Management for Paradise Realty

You work as a realtor for Paradise Realty, a small real estate agency located on Saltspring Island, the largest island in British Columbia's Gulf Islands region. You handle properties located throughout the islands, including Mayne Island, Galiano Island, Gabriola Island and, of course, Saltspring Island. Many of your clients e-mail you for information after viewing your listings on the company's Web site. In this project, you will use Outlook to create contacts for new clients and to organize your existing contacts.

Step 6
If the Journal icon does not appear on the Outlook bar, click Journal in the Folder List pane.

1. Create a contact for **Janice Alton** that appears as shown in Figure OP 4-1

2. In the Contacts folder, find the contact information for **Yves Torandot**, change his job title to **Senior Account Manager**, then flag the contact to call by **March 22, 2004** at **10:00 AM**

3. Create a new category called **Galiano Island**, then assign the following contacts to the Galiano Island category: **Harrison Chan, Dorothea Grunwald, Jamal Leblanc,** and **Wendy Paradou**
Now the Galiano Island category contains all of your clients who are interested in buying property on Galiano Island.

4. View the contacts in your contact list by **Company,** find the contacts from **North Vancouver Regional District,** then return to the default Address Cards view
Both Francis Oleander and Wendy Paradou work for the North Vancouver Regional District.

5. View the category associated with **Jamal Leblanc,** then add him to the Hot Contacts category
Jamal now belongs to both the Galiano Island and the Hot Contacts categories.

6. View **My Shortcuts** on the Outlook bar, then click the **Journal icon**

7. Create a new journal entry that appears as shown in Figure OP 4-2

8. Assign the journal entry to **Harrison Chan** and **Jamal LeBlanc**

9. Open the contact for **Harrison Chan,** then view the activity associated with him

Figure OP 4-1: Contact for Janice Alton

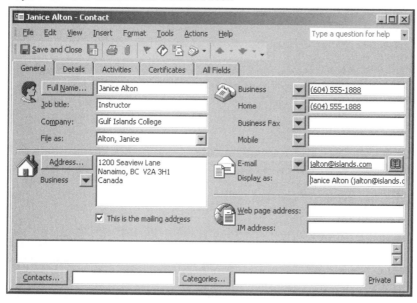

Figure OP 4-2: New journal entry

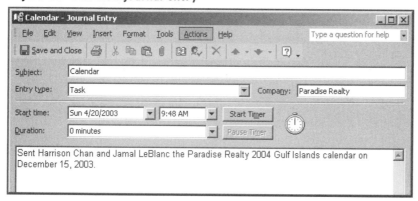

Project for Skill Set 5

Creating and Managing Tasks and Notes

Tasks and Notes for Step One Consulting

Step One Consulting holds full-day and weekend workshops in team building and leadership skills for companies in Dallas, Texas. As one of the company's seminar leaders, you will use Outlook in this project to keep track of your daily tasks and to receive tasks from and assign tasks to various co-workers.

1. As shown in Figure OP 5-1, create an **In Progress task** that starts on the current date and is due on tomorrow's date
   This task reminds you to call the caterers who will provide lunch and snacks for the upcoming leadership seminar for employees of Deer Lake Resort.

2. Open the **Web site updates task**, change the due date to tomorrow, change the status to **Waiting on someone else**, set the priority as **High**, set the recurrence to **Monthly**, and select the **Regenerate new task 1 month(s) after each task is completed** option button

Step 3
If a message appears telling you that the reminder has been turned off because the task no longer belongs to you, click OK.

3. Create a new task that includes **Seminar Materials** as the Subject and the message **Photocopy materials for the Deer Lake Resort seminar**, assign the new task to Sophia Jensen, set the due date as **tomorrow**, then send the request

4. Open the **Projector for May 3 Seminar** task, delegate the task to **Marcus Branson**, include the text **Can you take care of ordering the projector for your seminar?**, then send the request

5. Create the note shown in Figure OP 5-2, then assign the note to **Sophia Jensen**

6. Select the **May 10 Seminar** and the **June 3 Seminar** notes, then assign them to a new category called **Leadership Seminars**

Figure OP 5-1: Call caterers task

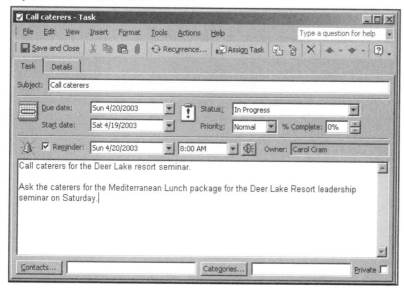

Figure OP 5-2: June seminars note

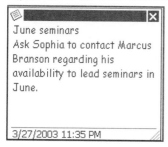

Glossary

Address Book A collection of names, addresses, phone numbers, and other information that can be used to quickly and easily address e-mail messages and keep track of people.

Answer Wizard tab A tab in the Help dialog box that lets you type a question or keyword in a box and search for related Help topics.

Appointment An Outlook item that is an activity, such as a meeting or phone call, that takes place on a specific day at a specific time.

Appointment area The section of the Calendar that resembles a yellow pad of paper and is divided into time slots where you can enter and view your appointments.

Appointment form A form where you enter detailed information about or make changes to a particular appointment.

Appointment tab The tab on the Meeting Request form used to enter details about a meeting, such as the subject, location, and invitees.

Archive A file for storing old Outlook items that you no longer want in your primary Outlook folders, but want to keep for future reference.

Ask a Question box A box at the right end of the Outlook menu bar into which you can type a question or keywords to access the Help system.

Attachment A file that is sent with an e-mail message to be downloaded or viewed by the recipient.

AutoArchive An Outlook feature that automatically removes files from your Inbox and other folders that you specify and places them in an archive file, where they are still accessible but out of the way.

AutoPreview A way of viewing messages in the Inbox. It displays the first three lines of every message.

Calendar The folder in Outlook used to store information about your schedule.

Category A keyword (or keywords) you can assign to an Outlook item. Categories make it possible to sort items into related groups.

Contact An entry in the Contacts folder that stores information about a particular person such as name, addresses, and phone numbers.

Contacts The folder in Outlook used to store information about people, such as names, addresses, phone numbers, and e-mail addresses.

Contents tab A tab in the Help dialog box that displays a comprehensive listing of all the Help topics available.

Date Navigator A small calendar located in the upper-right corner of the Calendar window. You can go to or display a date in any of the Calendar views by clicking it in the Date Navigator.

Deleted Items A folder in Outlook that stores items that have been removed using the Delete command

Dialog box A window from which you need to make selections or in which you need to type information in order for a task to be completed.

Drafts A folder in Outlook that stores in-progress e-mail messages that have not yet been sent.

e-mail Electronic mail messages transmitted over a computer network.

Event In Outlook, a full-day appointment.

Find bar A bar you open by clicking the Find button on the Standard toolbar. It lets you search for items by typing relevant keywords.

Folder A storage area on a computer disk used to organize files.

Folder banner A horizontal bar located just above the Outlook Bar in the Outlook program window that displays the name of the open folder.

Folder List A list that displays the folders and sub-folders available in Outlook.

Footer Text you can specify to print at the bottom of every page.

Full menu A menu that displays its entire available list of commands. To open a full menu, click the double arrows at the bottom of a short menu.

Header Text you can specify to print at the top of every page.

Index tab A tab in the Help dialog box that lets you search for Help topics by typing particular keywords.

Item A basic piece of information that is stored in an Outlook folder, such as an e-mail message or a Calendar appointment.

Journal A folder in Outlook that stores log entries that describe completed tasks or events that have occurred.

Journal entry An Outlook item that describes how you have spent time, such as the time spent completing a task or the results of a conference call.

Landscape A print orientation that prints a document in a wide format.

Meeting Request A type of e-mail message that requests the presence of the e-mail recipient at a meeting. A Meeting Request informs you of the location and subject of the meeting as well as the date and time. You can accept, decline, or propose a new meeting time for any Meeting Request you receive.

Meeting Request form A form used to invite attendees to a meeting.

Menu bar The bar located below the title bar of the Outlook program window that contains menu names. To open a menu, click a menu name.

Message form A window that displays the full text of an e-mail message and which you can use to write and send an e-mail message.

Note A computerized "sticky note" you can place anywhere on your screen as a reminder or note to yourself.

Note form The form you use to create Notes (computerized "sticky notes") in Outlook.

Notes A folder in Outlook that stores electronic "sticky notes" for recording thoughts, notes, ideas, and reminders.

Outbox A folder in Outlook that stores completed e-mail messages that have not yet been sent to the server for delivery.

Outlook Bar The bar along the left edge of the Outlook program window that contains icons for Outlook folders as well as shortcuts to My Computer, My Documents, Favorites, and other shortcuts you can specify.

Outlook Today folder The folder in Outlook that displays an at-a-glance view of the items in your Calendar, Tasks, and Inbox folders.

Outlook Update A folder in Outlook that opens the Microsoft Office Web site where you access resources, tools, and assistance for Outlook users.

Portrait A print orientation that prints a document in a tall format.

Preview pane A window that opens in the lower half of the View pane when the Inbox is open. It displays the text of the selected message.

Print style A format you choose for printing Outlook items. For example, Print styles for the Calendar include Daily, Weekly, and Monthly, among others.

Profile A group of e-mail accounts and address books set up for a particular user of Outlook.

Resource In Outlook, the name for a special piece of equipment such as a flip chart, monitor, or computer that you need to reserve for a meeting.

Scheduling tab The tab on the Meeting Request form used to view the schedules of all the meeting attendees and then set a meeting time that works for all.

Sent Items A folder in Outlook that stores e-mail messages that have been delivered.

Signature A block of information that is automatically appended to the end of an outgoing e-mail message.

Task An errand or activity you need to perform and that you can track through completion. Tasks are stored in the Tasks folder.

Task form A form you use to enter details about a particular task, including the subject, due date, and start date of the task.

TaskPad A window located in the lower-right corner of the Calendar window that displays a list of the tasks stored in your Tasks folder.

Tasks folder The folder in Outlook that stores information about to-do list items.

Text Only format A format you can save mail messages in that saves the text of a message but does not preserve the formatting of the original message.

Title bar The bar located at the top of the Outlook program window. It contains the name of the open folder or item, and the Minimize, (or Maximize), Restore, and Close buttons.

Toolbar A bar located just above the Folder banner that contains buttons you can click to perform tasks appropriate for the current folder.

View A particular way to display the items in an Outlook folder.

View pane The large area to the right of the Outlook Bar in the Outlook program window, where you view the contents of the current folder.

Voting buttons Buttons that appear in the Message form that let you quickly provide a response to an e-mail message. For instance, Yes/No voting buttons could be included in an e-mail message to make it easy for a recipient to respond quickly to a question.

Ways to Organize pane A window that lets you assign new or existing categories to your Outlook items.

Index

Ctrl R   Reply
Ctrl Shift R Reply all
Ctrl F   Forward

Ctrl E   Find